SELMA EVANS

ADHD
TOOLKIT
FOR
WOMEN

PROVEN STRATEGIES TO STRENGTHEN EXECUTIVE FUNCTIONING, OVERCOME ADHD CHALLENGES, AND SUCCEEDING BEYOND EXPECTATIONS

© **Copyright 2024 by Selma Evans - All rights reserved.**

The content contained within this book may not be reproduced, duplicated or transmitted without direct written permission from the author or the publisher.

Under no circumstances will any blame or legal responsibility be held against the publisher, or author, for any damages, reparation, or monetary loss due to the information contained within this book; either directly or indirectly.

Legal Notice:

This book is copyright protected. This book is only for personal use. You cannot amend, distribute, sell, use, quote or paraphrase any part, or the content within this book, without the consent of the author or publisher.

Disclaimer Notice:

Please note the information contained within this document is for educational and entertainment purposes only. All effort has been executed to present accurate, up-to-date, and reliable, complete information. No warranties of any kind are declared or implied. Readers acknowledge that the author is not engaging in the rendering of legal, financial, medical or professional advice.

ASIN: 979-12-81498-61-7

Contents

Introduction	1
Chapter 1: Understanding ADHD in Women	6
Chapter 2: Recognizing ADHD in Adult Women	25
Chapter 3: Emotional Aspects of ADHD	53
Chapter 4: ADHD in Daily Life	90
Chapter 5: Financial Management with ADHD	107
Chapter 6: Nurturing Relationships with ADHD	122
Chapter 7: Workplace Challenges and Strategies	142
Chapter 8: Fueling the ADHD Brain	156
Chapter 9: Harnessing Your Strengths	171
Conclusion	184

Introduction

Have you ever felt like you're living in a world that's just a step out of sync with you? Where your brain feels like a browser with too many tabs open, and you can't seem to close any of them? Welcome to the world of a woman with ADHD. It's a place where the simple things can feel overwhelmingly complex, and the complex things… well, they can feel nearly impossible.

Did you know that, according to recent studies, approximately 4% of adult women worldwide are living with ADHD? That's millions of women, each with her own story, challenges, and strengths. And yet, a staggering 50-75% of adult women with ADHD may remain undiagnosed. The reasons range from gender biases in diagnosis to the subtlety of symptoms in women.

This isn't just about numbers; it's about the lives behind them. Each statistic represents a woman like you, trying to navigate a world that often seems out of step with her unique way of thinking and being. These aren't just figures on a page; they're a reflection of a shared experience, a common struggle that connects us all.

For too long, our stories have been untold, our struggles unseen. We've lived in the shadows of misconceptions and stereotypes, trying to fit into a mold that just doesn't hold our shape. The constant juggle of work, life, and the myriad of expectations placed upon us can feel like a high-wire act with no safety net.

But here's the good news – you're not alone, and this book is your guide to navigating the waves of ADHD with grace and strength. Why should you keep turning these pages? Because within them lies a treasure trove of understanding, strategies, and real-life wisdom that speaks directly to your experiences. We're not just talking about dry facts and figures here. This is about real stories, practical advice, and a hearty dose of 'I get it' from people who truly understand what it's like to walk in your shoes.

We'll explore the unique ways ADHD manifests in women, how it's often hidden behind a mask of coping mechanisms and societal expectations. We'll delve into the daily battles – the lost keys, the missed appointments, the projects left unfinished – not to highlight the struggles, but to show you the paths to overcoming them.

Imagine having a guide that helps you turn your whirlwind of thoughts into a symphony of productivity. A guide that understands when your mind is racing at a million miles per hour and offers you the tools to slow it down, organize it, and make it work for you, not against you.

Here's what we're diving into: the real deal about women and ADHD. We'll debunk those old myths and show you how ADHD really plays out for us ladies. Hormones and ADHD? Yep, they're linked, and we'll explain how.

Big emotions, anxiety, the works – we've got practical tips for handling them all. Daily life can be a wild ride with ADHD, but we've got tricks for staying organized, managing time, and even sorting out money matters.

Relationships and work can be tricky with ADHD, but don't sweat it. We'll cover how to smooth things over and even use ADHD to your advantage at work. Plus, we'll dive into health tips, like diet and exercise, that make a difference.

Finding your tribe is important, and we'll guide you there. And the best part? We're celebrating the cool strengths that come with ADHD. This book is like your chat with a friend who gets it, packed with real advice for real life with ADHD.

This book is your invitation to a community that understands and accepts you just as you are. It's a journey towards self-discovery, where you'll learn not only to manage your symptoms but to embrace the unique strengths and talents that come with your ADHD. We're here to celebrate the creativity, the spontaneity, and the dynamic energy that ADHD brings into your life.

By the end of this book, you'll have a deeper understanding of your brain, a toolbox full of strategies for every aspect of your life, and most importantly, a renewed sense of confidence and empowerment. You'll see that ADHD is not a flaw, but a different way of thinking and being in the world – one that can be incredibly powerful when understood and harnessed correctly.

Ready for a fresh take? This book is like grabbing coffee with a friend who totally understands your ADHD rollercoaster. Forget medical jargon; it's all about real, relatable stories and tips that feel just right for you.

Time waits for no one, and neither should you. Every minute spent in the maze of ADHD without guidance is a minute too long. This isn't just another book to skim through; it's the key to unlocking a life where you're in control, not your ADHD. The journey ahead is urgent, necessary, and life-changing.

Think about it – how many times have you wished for answers, for a way to make sense of the chaos? Enough is enough. It's time to take back your life, to harness the whirlwind of your mind and turn it into your greatest asset.

This book is more than just words on a page; it's a call to action. It's your wake-up call to stop letting ADHD dictate your life. With each chapter, you'll gain not just knowledge, but power – the power to change, to grow, and to thrive. This is your moment to step up and say, 'I'm ready to transform my life.'

Don't wait for 'someday' or 'maybe.' The time to act is now. Your journey to mastering ADHD, to turning your challenges into triumphs, begins with the turn of this page. Are you ready to take this urgent, empowering step into a brighter, more manageable future? Let's do this. Together, right now, let's start rewriting your story.

Chapter 1: Understanding ADHD in Women

ADHD's been on our radar for ages, but the focus has primarily been on kids, especially boys. This skewed spotlight has left many women lurking in the shadows, misunderstood and often missing out on crucial diagnosis and support. It's high time to shed light on what ADHD really looks like for women – it's not just a male-dominated issue with a feminine twist. It's a complex interweaving of emotions and societal pressures that uniquely shape their experiences.

Ever feel like you're constantly trying to match up to everyone else's "normal," but no matter how hard you try, it just doesn't click? That's a day in the life for many women with ADHD. They struggle with what seems basic for others – staying organized, focused, and getting things done. This mismatch can significantly affect their sense of belonging and self-perception.

From childhood, girls with ADHD often become masters of disguise, learning to mimic their non-ADHD peers. This act of camouflage, while a survival mechanism, is draining and isolating. It leaves them feeling always a step away from being uncovered.

As they grow, the challenges evolve. Adulting adds layers of complexity, with pressures to juggle work, relationships, and perhaps parenting, all intertwined with ADHD. The male-centric narrative around ADHD has left countless women unaware of the root of their struggles until much later in life.

This lack of awareness isn't just a personal issue – it's a societal one. It leads to missed career opportunities, exacerbates the wage gap, and is a crucial element in the mental health crisis. Recognizing ADHD in women goes beyond identifying symptoms; it's about acknowledging a pervasive issue that affects every aspect of their lives.

Attention Deficit Hyperactivity Disorder (ADHD) is a neurodevelopmental disorder characterized by inattention, hyperactivity, and impulsivity. The impact of ADHD varies widely, shaped by factors like symptom severity, co-occurring disorders, and environmental influences.

ADHD manifests in three main types:

- **Predominantly Inattentive Type**: Challenges include maintaining attention and organization, often leading to difficulties in academic or occupational settings.

- **Predominantly Hyperactive-Impulsive Type**: Characterized by excessive fidgeting and impulsive actions, causing issues in environments requiring calm behavior.

- **Combined Type**: Involves both inattentive and hyperactive-impulsive symptoms, presenting challenges across various life domains.

The spectrum of ADHD functioning, described as "high-functioning" and "low-functioning," reflects the diverse experiences of individuals with ADHD. Women with "high-functioning" ADHD may effectively manage their symptoms but still face internal challenges. Those with "low-functioning" ADHD experience more pronounced difficulties, often needing more support.

Understanding ADHD's impact involves looking at several key factors: the intensity of symptoms, co-existing mental health conditions, the available support network, personal coping methods, and the surrounding environment. Grasping these aspects is key to fully understanding ADHD, particularly in the context of women's experiences, and addressing the broader societal challenges associated with this often misunderstood condition. As we move forward, we'll explore these elements in greater detail. But first, let's step back and look at the bigger picture. I want to provide a wider lens on ADHD, exploring its growth and unique impact in the lives of women. That's where our journey begins.

Genetics and How the Brain Works

Tackling ADHD is like putting together a massive puzzle that combines bits of science, genetics, and a few unknowns. We're on this fascinating journey to piece together why ADHD happens by exploring the mix of genes, brain activity, and environmental factors. It's quite the adventure, really, trying to get a handle on this complex condition.

Front and center in this quest are genetics. Yep, ADHD can run in families, kind of like inheriting your mom's knack for storytelling or your granddad's eye color. It's like this family trait that's passed around, but no one really chats about it much. You might notice it more than you'd think at family gatherings, showing just how big a role our genes play in ADHD.

Scientists have been busy bees, identifying specific genes linked to ADHD. This tells us that ADHD isn't about one lone gene going rogue but involves a bunch of genes teaming up in intricate ways. Some of the key players include genes like DRD4 and DRD5, which are all about how our brains deal with dopamine, crucial for keeping our attention and behaviors in check. Then there's DAT1, affecting dopamine transport and playing into how focused or impulsive we might be. And don't forget about ADRA2A, which impacts how norepinephrine helps us stay alert and rein in those impulses.

But here's the thing—it's super complicated. Having certain versions of these genes doesn't mean someone will definitely have ADHD, nor does it mean they can't manage well. It's not all in the genes, either. Stuff like how you were raised, what you've been exposed to, and even your diet can influence ADHD. The deep dive into ADHD's genetic side is all about getting a clearer picture of the condition, hopefully leading to treatments that are more tailored to each person.

So, while this genetic exploration is a piece of the puzzle, it's crucial to remember that managing ADHD is about looking at the whole picture, including the environment we grow up and live in. The aim is to better understand ADHD, making way for strategies that really hit the mark for those navigating this condition.

Spotting the Subtle Signs: ADHD in Girls

When it comes to ADHD, boys often steal the spotlight—not because they're more susceptible by nature, but because their symptoms tend to be louder and more visible. Girls, on the other hand, can fly under the radar with their version of ADHD, making it a sneaky guest that's hard to spot. Let's break down the early signs and symptoms in girls, which can be quite the chameleons, blending into the backdrop of everyday behaviors and societal expectations.

Inattentiveness

First up, we've got inattentiveness. But we're not talking about the occasional daydreaming when class gets boring. Girls with ADHD might find it tough to stick with tasks that don't spark an immediate interest. It's like their mind is a TV with someone else holding the remote, flipping channels when they're supposed to be watching a specific show. This can lead to trouble following instructions or completing tasks, as their brain is off on a mini-adventure elsewhere.

Hyperfocus

Then there's the paradox of hyperfocus. Yep, the same kids who can't seem to pay attention to a 10-minute homework assignment might lose themselves for hours in activities they love. It's like their attention span has an on-off switch with no in-between. This hyperfocus can be a superpower in the right context but also means important stuff can get neglected in the meantime.

Impulsivity

Impulsivity in girls with ADHD might not always mean running around the classroom. It's more subtle, like blurting out answers without being called on or making quick decisions without stopping to think about the outcomes. It's a bit like jumping into a pool without checking if there's water in it—risky and sometimes messy.

Emotional Sensitivity

Emotional sensitivity is another key sign. Life for a girl with ADHD can feel like being on an emotional rollercoaster without a seatbelt. They might have intense reactions to situations that others see as minor, which can quickly get labeled as moodiness or being overly sensitive. It's not drama; it's their brain's amplified response to the world around them.

Social Challenges

Lastly, we've got the social challenges. Making and keeping friends can be a tough puzzle for girls with ADHD. They might miss subtle social cues, find it hard to keep up with group conversations, or struggle to play the social game by unspoken rules. It's like being at a dance where everyone knows the steps except you.

Stepping into Adulthood

Moving into adulthood, women with ADHD face a whole new set of challenges that go way beyond the classroom drama and social mazes of their teenage years. This phase brings new arenas—career, relationships, self-management—where ADHD continues to be a significant player, often making women navigate through a complex web of expectations and responsibilities.

Career and Workplace Dynamics

Jumping into the career pool, women with ADHD often find themselves caught between a rock and a hard place. On one hand, the professional world is full of pitfalls like organizational hurdles, time management traps, and multitasking labyrinths that can make keeping focus feel like an uphill battle. The high demand for attention to detail and juggling multiple tasks in fast-paced jobs can feel like being tossed into the deep end, especially when positive feedback is as scarce as sunny days in London.

But it's not all gloomy. Many women find that the very traits that challenge them in the workplace also arm them with a unique skill set. Their knack for thinking outside the box, tackling problems from creative angles, and channeling hyperfocus moments can make them standout players in the right roles. Discovering that sweet spot where ADHD's inventive and dynamic qualities are valued rather than suppressed can be like finding treasure.

Relationships and Family Life

When it comes to relationships and family dynamics, the plot thickens. The same hurdles that once complicated teenage friendships—like navigating communication snags and emotional whirlwinds—don't just disappear; they evolve. Adult relationships, whether with partners or children, introduce their own dramas and joys. Balancing the whirlwind of family responsibilities, with its endless to-do list, against the backdrop of ADHD can sometimes feel like performing a circus act.

It's a fine line, trying to be a supportive partner or a patient parent while managing ADHD's quirks. The pressure to check off all the boxes of perfection amplifies every slip-up, turning moments of doubt into mountains. Yet, these challenges also pave the way for growth, deeper understanding, and stronger bonds built on patience and mutual respect.

Self-Management and Self-Care

And then there's the personal journey of self-management and self-care, perhaps the most intimate battleground. Keeping the ship sailing smoothly when your brain loves to throw curveballs is no small task. From perfecting daily routines to steering through the stormy waters of personal finances, it's a constant learning process.

Not to mention the health trifecta: diet, exercise, and sleep. In a world where maintaining a healthy lifestyle can feel like solving a puzzle, impulsivity and shifting motivation levels add extra pieces to the mix. Crafting a balanced life amid these dynamics is an ongoing adventure, one that calls for kindness, perseverance, and sometimes, a good sense of humor to navigate the chaos.

Mental Health Matters

Mental health emerges not just as a topic of interest but as a central theme, especially for women with ADHD. The journey through adulthood, with its myriad responsibilities and challenges, can often amplify feelings of anxiety, give rise to episodes of depression, and test the resilience of one's self-esteem. For many women, reaching adulthood marks a pivotal moment—a time when the full weight of years spent wrestling with ADHD's complexities truly becomes apparent.

The ebb and flow of daily life can, for some, feel like navigating through a storm with no harbor in sight. Anxiety, for instance, might not just be a fleeting feeling of nervousness but a constant hum in the background, turning what should be simple decisions into mountains of worry. It's like living with a soundtrack of concerns that plays on loop, making it hard to find a moment's peace. Whether it's fretting over deadlines at work, managing household tasks, or maintaining social connections, the presence of ADHD can turn these routine stresses into sources of overwhelming anxiety.

Depression, too, can sneak in, often disguised as mere exhaustion or a temporary funk. But for those with ADHD, it can develop into a more persistent shadow, darkening the brighter aspects of life. It's akin to walking through life with a filter that dims the joy and amplifies the challenges, making even small setbacks feel like insurmountable failures. This can be particularly challenging when past efforts to overcome ADHD-related obstacles have been met with frustration or misunderstanding, leading to feelings of isolation or hopelessness.

Self-esteem, the very foundation upon which we build our sense of self-worth and confidence, can be particularly vulnerable. The trials and tribulations associated with ADHD—missteps in social settings, academic or professional challenges, and the daily struggle to manage symptoms—can chip away at one's self-image. It's as though each hurdle encountered and each goal that feels just out of reach serves to reinforce a narrative of inadequacy, despite the countless victories and moments of resilience that go unnoticed.

In the face of these mental health challenges, the importance of a robust support network cannot be overstated. Friends, family, and peers who understand and empathize with the ADHD experience can provide a lifeline, offering encouragement and a reminder that one is not alone in this journey. Therapy, too, plays a vital role, offering a space for guidance, healing, and the development of strategies tailored to navigate the complexities of ADHD. A therapist who specializes in ADHD can help untangle the web of feelings, behaviors, and thoughts, providing clarity and a path forward.

Self-kindness emerges as a powerful ally in this context. Cultivating an attitude of compassion towards oneself, recognizing the efforts made rather than just the outcomes, and celebrating the small victories can foster a sense of resilience and hope. It's about shifting the focus from what hasn't been achieved to appreciating the strength it takes to face each day with ADHD. Engaging in self-care practices, whether through mindfulness, exercise, hobbies, or simply allowing for moments of rest, becomes an act of rebellion against the inner critic that thrives on doubt and criticism.

Dispelling Myths and Stereotypes

Before we advance to the subsequent chapter, it's essential to correct some widespread misunderstandings. A myriad of myths surround Attention Deficit Hyperactivity Disorder in women, causing confusion, incorrect diagnoses, and a lack of necessary treatment. These misconceptions not only foster stigma but also hinder affected individuals from pursuing and obtaining the correct support. Let's address and dispel some of the most prevalent myths regarding ADHD in women:

1. **Myth: ADHD is a Condition Only Affecting Men and Boys.**

    ◦ Reality: ADHD affects both genders. Women and girls are often underdiagnosed due to differences in how symptoms present, societal expectations, and a historical bias towards studying ADHD in males.

2. **Myth: Women with ADHD are Just Naturally Disorganized and Emotional.**

    ◦ Reality: While disorganization and emotional sensitivity can be characteristics of ADHD, they are not simply personality traits. These are symptoms of a neurological disorder that impacts various aspects of life and functioning.

3. **Myth: ADHD Symptoms in Women are Always Visible.**

    ◦ Reality: ADHD in women often manifests in less overt ways compared to men. Symptoms like inattentiveness, internal restlessness, and emotional dysregulation can be less visible and are often internalized.

4. **Myth: Women with ADHD Cannot be Successful.**

    ◦ Reality: Women with ADHD can be highly successful in various fields. With the right support, strategies, and accommodations, they can manage symptoms and leverage their strengths, such as creativity and problem-solving abilities.

5. **Myth: ADHD in Women is Just Hormonal or Mood Issues.**

    ◦ Reality: While hormonal fluctuations can impact ADHD symptoms, ADHD itself is a distinct neurodevelopmental disorder. It's not solely a result of hormonal changes or mood disorders, though these can coexist with ADHD.

6. **Myth: If You Did Well in School, You Don't Have ADHD.**

- Reality: Many women with ADHD develop coping mechanisms that allow them to excel academically. High intelligence and creativity can mask ADHD symptoms, leading to late diagnosis.

7. **Myth: ADHD Medication is Less Effective in Women.**

   - Reality: ADHD medications can be effective for both men and women. However, hormonal changes may affect medication efficacy, so women may require tailored treatment plans.

8. **Myth: ADHD is Overdiagnosed in Women Seeking an Excuse for Laziness.**

   - Reality: ADHD is often underdiagnosed in women. Those who seek diagnosis and treatment are looking for explanations and strategies to manage their symptoms, not excuses for their challenges.

9. **Myth: Women Outgrow ADHD.**

   - Reality: ADHD is a lifelong condition. While symptoms may change over time, many women continue to experience them into adulthood. Treatment and coping strategies may need to be adjusted throughout different life stages.

10. **Myth: Only Hyperactive Boys Have ADHD, So Girls Must Be Fine.**

    ○ Reality: ADHD presents in three types: primarily hyperactive-impulsive, primarily inattentive, and combined. Women and girls are more often diagnosed with the primarily inattentive type, which can be less conspicuous and, therefore, overlooked.

Highlights of The Chapter

ADHD in women has been overlooked for too long, often masked by societal expectations and a focus on the disorder's more visible manifestations in boys. This oversight leaves many women struggling in silence, wrestling with a disorder that impacts every aspect of their lives, from childhood through adulthood. Women with ADHD frequently grapple with feelings of inadequacy as they strive to meet the seemingly effortless standards set by their peers, leading to a lifetime of compensating and camouflaging their difficulties.

The journey for women with ADHD is fraught with challenges that evolve over time. In their youth, girls may develop sophisticated masking techniques to blend in, a strategy that, while effective in avoiding detection, can lead to isolation and mental exhaustion. As they transition into adulthood, the stakes are raised with the added complexities of professional responsibilities, personal relationships, and the potential of parenthood, all intertwined with the constant struggle to manage ADHD symptoms.

The societal narrative around ADHD exacerbates the issue, with pervasive myths and misconceptions about the disorder contributing to delayed diagnoses and inadequate support. This narrative often paints ADHD as a condition of disorganization and emotional instability, ignoring the neurological underpinnings and the diverse manifestations of the disorder. Women with ADHD might not only face challenges in maintaining focus and organization but also navigate a world that misunderstands and undervalues their experiences.

Key Points:

- **Beyond the Boy-Centric View**: ADHD in women has been shadowed by a focus on boys, neglecting how the disorder differently affects women and leads to underdiagnosis.

- **The Camouflage Effect**: From an early age, girls with ADHD learn to mask their symptoms to fit societal norms, a survival tactic that comes with a cost to their mental health and self-esteem.

- **Adult Life Complexity**: The transition to adulthood introduces new layers of challenge for women with ADHD, complicating career paths, relationships, and self-management in ways that can magnify their struggles.

- **Mental Health Intersection**: ADHD in women often coexists with anxiety, depression, and emotional dysregulation, underscoring the need for a holistic approach to support and treatment.

- **Dispelling Harmful Myths**: Addressing and debunking myths about ADHD in women is crucial for improving awareness, diagnosis, and support. These myths, including misconceptions about the visibility of symptoms and the ability to achieve success, hinder understanding and proper care.

- **The Importance of Tailored Support**: Recognizing the unique challenges faced by women with ADHD calls for personalized strategies in treatment and support, acknowledging the diverse ways in which ADHD manifests and impacts their lives.

- **Recognizing Strengths Amid Challenges**: Despite the hurdles, many women with ADHD harness their unique perspectives and creativity, turning perceived weaknesses into strengths in the right environments.

Chapter 2: Recognizing ADHD in Adult Women

Attention-Deficit/Hyperactivity Disorder, more commonly known as ADHD, stands as a multifaceted neurodevelopmental disorder that doesn't discriminate based on gender. It can influence the lives of individuals far and wide, impacting their daily functioning, relationships, and self-perception. Yet, despite its wide-reaching effects, the journey of living with ADHD can differ markedly between genders. This chapter aims to peel back the layers of these differences, offering a deep dive into how ADHD manifests uniquely in women compared to men, the challenges surrounding diagnosis, and the societal perceptions that play a significant role in these disparities.

Historically, ADHD has been stereotypically associated with hyperactive young boys, causing a significant oversight in recognizing the condition in girls and women. This oversight is not just a simple misstep but a profound reflection of the gender biases ingrained in our diagnostic systems and societal understanding. Women with ADHD often experience symptoms that are less overt and more internalized than their male counterparts. Symptoms such as inattentiveness, daydreaming, and emotional dysregulation are common, yet they are frequently overlooked or misattributed to personality quirks, mood disorders, or simply being labelled as "too emotional."

The path to diagnosis for women is often fraught with hurdles, compounded by a lack of awareness and understanding among healthcare professionals about how ADHD presents in females. This delay in diagnosis can lead to years of misunderstanding one's own experiences, leading to secondary issues such as low self-esteem, anxiety, and depression. Furthermore, societal expectations placed on women to be organized, nurturing, and composed amplify the internal struggle of those with ADHD, as they may feel they fall short of these prescribed roles.

Moreover, the societal lens through which women with ADHD are viewed and treated adds another layer of complexity. The narrative around ADHD needs to shift from a one-size-fits-all perspective to a more nuanced understanding that respects and recognizes the diversity in ADHD presentations. Acknowledging this diversity is the first step towards fostering a more inclusive and supportive environment for all individuals with ADHD.

This chapter aims to explore these themes in detail, providing insights into the nuanced ways in which ADHD affects women. From the subtle signs of ADHD in women that often go unnoticed to the systemic barriers that hinder their diagnosis and treatment, we'll delve into the societal perceptions that contribute to these disparities.

Understanding ADHD Across Genders

Delving deeper into the realm of ADHD and its intersection with gender, it becomes evident that our comprehension of the disorder has been skewed by a historical focus on male-dominated research and narratives. This gender bias in the foundational understanding of ADHD has led to a narrow view of how symptoms present themselves, often overlooking or misinterpreting them in women. The broad categorization of ADHD symptoms into two primary types—Inattentive Type and Hyperactive-Impulsive Type—provides a framework for diagnosis, yet the nuances of gender can significantly influence the manifestation and recognition of these symptoms.

In women, ADHD symptoms often lean more towards the Inattentive Type. These symptoms include difficulty maintaining focus, being easily distracted, forgetfulness in daily activities, and problems organizing tasks. Unlike the more visible Hyperactive-Impulsive symptoms, such as fidgeting, interrupting, and an inability to stay seated, the inattentive symptoms can be subtle and easily mistaken for disinterest, laziness, or even a lack of intelligence. This misunderstanding is further compounded by societal expectations that women should be naturally adept at juggling multiple tasks and responsibilities. When women with ADHD struggle in these areas, they are not only misinterpreted through the lens of ADHD symptoms but also through the critical lens of failing gender norms.

The gender bias in ADHD research and diagnosis has profound implications for women. For decades, the narrative surrounding ADHD has been so closely aligned with hyperactivity and impulsiveness—traits more socially acceptable or expected in boys—that when girls or women exhibit primarily inattentive symptoms, they are often overlooked. This oversight means that many women with ADHD reach adulthood without a diagnosis, having navigated their formative years feeling out of place, misunderstood, or criticized for traits that are inherent to their neurodevelopmental makeup.

Moreover, this bias in understanding ADHD across genders extends into the realm of treatment and support. The lack of gender-specific research and resources means that women are often navigating a treatment landscape that has been predominantly designed with men in mind. This one-size-fits-all approach to treatment can overlook the unique challenges women with ADHD face, such as hormonal fluctuations that can exacerbate symptoms or the societal pressures that compound the impact of ADHD on their mental health.

The Invisibility of ADHD in Women

The phenomenon of ADHD's invisibility in women is a complex issue that stems from the subtler, less visible presentation of symptoms predominantly associated with the Inattentive Type of ADHD. Unlike the Hyperactive-Impulsive Type, which manifests in ways that are hard to ignore—such as constant movement, impulsive actions, and difficulty waiting turns—the Inattentive Type presents with symptoms that blend into societal expectations of femininity or are dismissed as mere personality quirks. Daydreaming, a propensity for being easily distracted, struggles with maintaining focus on tasks, and disorganization are hallmark signs of inattentive ADHD. Yet, these symptoms are often overlooked by educators, family members, and even healthcare professionals, or worse, misattributed to a lack of effort, disinterest, or the nebulous concept of a "spacey" personality.

This oversight is not a minor issue but a significant barrier to recognition and diagnosis for women with ADHD. The invisibility of their symptoms leads to a profound misunderstanding of their experiences, contributing to a cycle of underdiagnosis or delayed diagnosis. It's not uncommon for women to reach their adult years—sometimes only seeking help for their ADHD after their children are diagnosed—before they receive a diagnosis themselves. This delay means that women spend years, if not decades, without the understanding or support needed to navigate their ADHD effectively.

The subtlety of inattentive symptoms and their misinterpretation as personality traits rather than indicators of a neurodevelopmental disorder significantly impact women's self-esteem and mental health. Without recognition of the root cause of their struggles, women are often left feeling inadequate, blaming themselves for their perceived shortcomings in organizational skills, time management, and focus. The societal expectation for women to excel in roles requiring high levels of organization and multitasking further exacerbates these feelings, creating a cycle of self-doubt and frustration.

Moreover, the invisibility of ADHD in women contributes to a lack of tailored support and resources. As most research and therapeutic interventions have historically centered on the more visible Hyperactive-Impulsive Type, commonly observed in boys and men, there is a significant gap in approaches specifically designed to address the unique challenges faced by women with the Inattentive Type of ADHD. This gap underscores the urgent need for a shift in both awareness and clinical practice to recognize and accommodate the distinct experiences of women with ADHD.

Addressing the invisibility of ADHD in women requires a multifaceted approach. It necessitates increased awareness and education about the gender-specific manifestations of ADHD, both within the medical community and society at large. Educators, healthcare providers, and families must be equipped with the knowledge to identify the less overt symptoms of ADHD in girls and women. Additionally, there's a critical need for research that focuses on ADHD in women, to develop diagnostic criteria and treatment strategies that reflect the nuances of how the disorder presents across genders.

The Role of Hormones in ADHD

The intersection of hormones and ADHD in women represents a pivotal yet underexplored dimension of how the disorder manifests and fluctuates across different life stages. Hormonal changes, inherent to women's reproductive cycles, have a profound impact on ADHD symptoms, often exacerbating them during key hormonal milestones such as puberty, menstruation, pregnancy, and menopause. This dynamic adds a layer of complexity to both the diagnosis and management of ADHD in women, underscoring the critical need for a deeper understanding and more nuanced approach in medical research and practice.

During puberty, the surge of hormones can intensify ADHD symptoms, making this already tumultuous phase even more challenging for young girls. The hormonal rollercoaster does not only contribute to emotional volatility but can also aggravate the core symptoms of ADHD, such as inattention, distractibility, and impulsivity. This exacerbation can significantly impact academic performance and social interactions, pivotal areas of development during adolescence.

The menstrual cycle further illustrates the impact of hormonal fluctuations on ADHD. Many women report a worsening of their symptoms in the premenstrual phase when estrogen levels drop. This period can be marked by heightened emotional sensitivity, increased impulsivity, and a noticeable decline in executive functioning, making tasks that require organization, focus, and self-regulation more difficult. Despite these observable patterns, the conversation around menstruation and its impact on ADHD remains surprisingly limited in both clinical settings and public discourse.

Pregnancy and the postpartum period introduce another phase of significant hormonal changes, with varying effects on ADHD symptoms. Some women experience a temporary alleviation of their symptoms during pregnancy, likely due to increased estrogen levels, while others may notice no change or even a worsening of symptoms. The postpartum period, with its rapid hormonal shifts, poses a risk for increased ADHD symptoms alongside the potential for mood disorders, complicating the already challenging transition to motherhood.

Menopause represents yet another critical juncture where hormonal fluctuations can influence ADHD. The decline in estrogen during perimenopause and menopause can lead to an increase in ADHD symptoms, coupled with the challenges of navigating menopausal symptoms such as hot flashes, sleep disturbances, and mood swings. The overlap of these symptoms can make the management of ADHD more complex, requiring adjustments in treatment strategies to accommodate these changes.

Despite the clear link between hormonal fluctuations and the exacerbation of ADHD symptoms in women, this area remains under-researched and inadequately addressed in clinical practice. The lack of awareness and understanding about the role of hormones in ADHD contributes to gaps in diagnosis, treatment, and support for women at various stages of their life. Addressing this gap requires a concerted effort in medical research to investigate the hormonal aspects of ADHD comprehensively. Clinicians need to be mindful of the hormonal influences on

ADHD when diagnosing and treating women, incorporating questions about menstrual cycles, pregnancy, and menopause into their assessments.

The Path to Diagnosis

The path to receiving an ADHD diagnosis for many women is often long, winding, and fraught with obstacles. This challenging journey is largely due to persistent misunderstandings and stereotypes about ADHD, particularly regarding how the disorder manifests differently across genders. Women seeking diagnosis frequently encounter skepticism, misdiagnosis, or outright dismissal from healthcare providers, a disheartening experience that can significantly impede their access to necessary support and treatment.

Misdiagnosis is a common issue, with women often being incorrectly diagnosed with anxiety, depression, or bipolar disorder instead of ADHD. This misattribution of symptoms not only delays the receipt of appropriate care but can also lead to treatment plans that are ineffective or even counterproductive. Moreover, the experience of having one's concerns invalidated or misunderstood by professionals can be deeply discouraging, leading many women to internalize their struggles or give up on seeking help altogether.

The Role of Self-Assessment Tools

Self-assessment tools for ADHD are widely available and can be a helpful starting point for individuals suspecting they might have ADHD. These tools typically consist of questionnaires designed to gauge the frequency and severity of symptoms associated with ADHD. They often cover areas like attention span, impulsivity, organization skills, time management, and emotional regulation. (I have included a self-assessment test at the end of the chapter)

While these tools are primarily meant to provide an initial insight into whether your experiences align with common ADHD symptoms, it's important to understand that they are not diagnostic. ADHD is a complex disorder that overlaps with various other conditions, and a thorough evaluation by a mental health professional is necessary for a diagnosis.

Transitioning to Professional Diagnosis

After self-assessment, the next crucial step is seeking a professional diagnosis. This process involves a detailed evaluation by a qualified healthcare provider, such as a psychologist, psychiatrist, or neurologist who specializes in ADHD.

A professional diagnosis typically involves a review of the individual's complete medical history, behavioral observations, and possibly interviews with family members or significant others. Healthcare providers might use a combination of diagnostic tools, including structured interviews, rating scales, and sometimes, neuropsychological testing. They are trained to distinguish ADHD from other mental health conditions like anxiety or mood disorders, which can present similar symptoms. This differentiation is crucial for effective treatment planning.

Navigating the Diagnostic Process

The process of getting diagnosed can be daunting, especially for adults who might have lived with undiagnosed ADHD for years. It's important to approach this process with patience and an open mind. Preparing for the appointment, gathering information about your symptoms and how they impact your life can be helpful. Communication is key: be honest and thorough in sharing your experiences and concerns with the healthcare provider. After the diagnosis, remember that a diagnosis is a step towards understanding yourself better and managing your life more effectively.

Tailored Treatment Approaches

Tailored treatment approaches that take gender differences into account are crucial for women with ADHD. These approaches should consider the challenges of managing symptoms in the context of societal expectations, dealing with the effects of hormonal changes, and balancing the disorder with family and work responsibilities. A one-size-fits-all approach to treatment is insufficient; healthcare providers must consider these factors when developing treatment plans, which could include a combination of medication, cognitive-behavioral therapy, coaching, and support groups.

ADHD and Co-occurring Conditions

ADHD rarely travels alone. It often comes hand-in-hand with one or more co-occurring conditions, also known as comorbidities. These can be other mental health disorders, learning disabilities, or even physical health issues. The presence of these additional conditions can muddy the waters of diagnosis and treatment, making it harder to pinpoint ADHD and address it effectively.

Common Co-occurring Mental Health Disorders

- **Anxiety Disorders**: The coexistence of ADHD and anxiety disorders is a common clinical scenario. For many with ADHD, the continual challenges in organizing tasks, remembering important information, and meeting deadlines can be a significant source of anxiety. This anxiety, in turn, can further impair their ability to concentrate and manage their ADHD symptoms, creating a feedback loop that exacerbates both conditions. The pervasive sense of being overwhelmed can lead to a constant state of tension and worry, significantly impacting daily functioning and quality of life.

- **Depression**: Depression frequently accompanies ADHD, often as a secondary condition. The repeated difficulties and setbacks experienced by individuals with ADHD—such as chronic disorganization, underachievement, and relationship challenges—can take a toll on self-esteem and lead to feelings of hopelessness and low self-worth. This emotional toll can manifest as depression, characterized by persistent sadness, loss of interest in previously enjoyed activities, and a general sense of despair. It's important to recognize that in individuals with ADHD, depression may not only be a comorbid condition but also a reaction to the continual struggles and frustrations associated with managing their ADHD.

- **Bipolar Disorder**: Distinguishing between ADHD and bipolar disorder can be particularly challenging due to the overlap in symptoms. Both disorders can feature high energy levels, impulsivity, and periods of heightened activity. However, bipolar disorder is characterized by episodes of mania or hypomania, typically involving elevated mood, grandiosity, and extreme increases in activity or energy, interspersed with episodes of depression. This cyclical pattern is distinct from the consistent symptomatology of ADHD. Accurate diagnosis is crucial as the treatment for bipolar disorder differs significantly from that of ADHD.

- **Personality Disorders**: There is also a noted overlap between ADHD and certain personality disorders, such as borderline personality disorder (BPD). Both ADHD and BPD can share traits such as impulsivity, mood instability, and challenges in maintaining stable relationships. However, BPD is characterized by a pattern of intense and unstable interpersonal relationships, a marked and persistent fear of abandonment, identity disturbance, and recurrent suicidal behavior or self-harm. The overlapping symptoms can sometimes lead to misdiagnosis or an incomplete understanding of the individual's psychological profile.

Learning Disabilities and ADHD

Learning disabilities frequently co-occur with ADHD, adding another dimension of challenge to the educational and professional experiences of those affected. Conditions like dyslexia and dyscalculia are particularly common among individuals with ADHD. The presence of these learning disabilities alongside ADHD necessitates a nuanced understanding and tailored approach to both education and workplace environments.

1. **Dyslexia**: Dyslexia, characterized by difficulties with accurate and/or fluent word recognition, poor spelling, and decoding abilities, often coexists with ADHD. For individuals with both ADHD and dyslexia, the challenges in maintaining focus and attention exacerbate the difficulties in processing and comprehending written text. This dual impact can make academic tasks particularly strenuous, often leading to a slower pace in learning, reading, and completing assignments. The frustration and effort required to overcome these hurdles can also affect self-esteem and motivation.

2. **Dyscalculia**: Dyscalculia, a specific learning disability in mathematics, is another condition that can co-occur with ADHD. It involves challenges in understanding numbers, learning how to manipulate numbers, performing mathematical calculations, and learning math facts. When combined with ADHD, individuals may struggle not only with the inherent difficulties of dyscalculia but also with the attentional demands of mathematical tasks. This can result in significant challenges in academic environments, especially in subjects

requiring sustained mental effort and precision.

The co-occurrence of learning disabilities and ADHD calls for specialized learning strategies and accommodations. In educational settings, this might include individualized education plans (IEPs), extra time on tests, tutoring, or the use of assistive technology. These accommodations are designed to address both the attentional challenges of ADHD and the specific learning difficulties posed by conditions like dyslexia or dyscalculia.

In professional settings, similar accommodations can be made to support individuals with ADHD and learning disabilities. This might involve providing written instructions, allowing for flexible work hours to manage focus and energy levels, or implementing organizational tools and technology to aid task management.

Early identification and intervention are key in managing the combination of ADHD and learning disabilities. Specialized educational support, such as structured literacy programs for dyslexia or math intervention programs for dyscalculia, can be highly beneficial. Moreover, psychoeducational testing can be crucial in identifying the specific learning challenges and tailoring the interventions accordingly.

Furthermore, fostering an environment of understanding and support is essential. Educators, employers, and peers need to be aware of the challenges faced by individuals with ADHD and learning disabilities. Building this awareness can lead to more empathetic and supportive relationships, both academically and professionally.

Physical Health Conditions

The relationship between ADHD and physical health conditions presents yet another layer of complexity in understanding and managing the disorder. Commonly associated physical health issues, such as sleep disorders, obesity, and substance abuse, not only have a direct impact on overall well-being but also interact with ADHD symptoms in ways that can exacerbate the disorder.

   1. **Sleep Disorders**: Individuals with ADHD often experience sleep-related issues, including difficulty falling asleep, restless sleep, and waking up frequently during the night. These sleep disturbances can stem from the hyperarousal and difficulty in winding down commonly associated with ADHD. Poor sleep quality and quantity can significantly worsen ADHD symptoms, particularly inattention and impulsivity, creating a challenging cycle where sleep issues and ADHD

symptoms mutually reinforce each other.

2. **Obesity**: There is a notable link between ADHD and obesity. The impulsivity and poor planning skills associated with ADHD can contribute to unhealthy eating behaviors, such as binge eating or a preference for high-calorie, low-nutrient foods. Additionally, the challenges in maintaining a routine or following through with plans can make it difficult for individuals with ADHD to stick to a healthy diet or exercise regimen. This connection highlights the importance of addressing lifestyle and dietary habits as part of a comprehensive approach to managing ADHD.

3. **Substance Abuse**: The propensity for impulsivity and risk-taking behaviors in individuals with ADHD can increase the likelihood of substance abuse. This may manifest as self-medicating with alcohol or drugs as a way to cope with the symptoms of ADHD or the stress and challenges it brings. Substance abuse, in turn, can further complicate the symptoms of ADHD and interfere with its treatment, creating a detrimental cycle that can be hard to break.

Addressing these physical health conditions in the context of ADHD requires a multifaceted approach. For sleep disorders, interventions might include practicing good sleep hygiene, possibly using medication to regulate sleep patterns, and behavioral strategies to manage the hyperarousal symptoms of ADHD. In the case of obesity, a combination of dietary counseling, structured exercise programs, and addressing the impulsive behaviors related to eating can be effective.

For substance abuse issues, it is crucial to provide comprehensive support that addresses both the substance use and the underlying ADHD. This could involve therapy, support groups, and possibly medication to manage ADHD symptoms, reducing the individual's need to self-medicate.

In managing these physical health conditions alongside ADHD, a holistic view of the individual's health is essential. Healthcare providers should consider how ADHD contributes to these physical health issues and vice versa. By doing so, they can develop more effective treatment plans that address the full range of challenges faced by individuals with ADHD. This comprehensive approach not only improves ADHD symptoms but also enhances overall physical health and quality of life.

The Diagnostic Challenge

The key to overcoming these diagnostic challenges lies in a comprehensive and holistic assessment process. Mental health professionals should conduct a thorough evaluation that encompasses a detailed clinical history, symptom analysis, and an assessment of functional impairment across various settings (such as home, school, or work). This may include:

- **Clinical Interviews**: In-depth discussions with the patient, and when appropriate, family members or significant others, to gather a comprehensive history and understanding of the symptoms' nature and impact.

- **Standardized Rating Scales**: Utilizing ADHD-specific assessment tools and scales can help quantify symptoms and differentiate them from those of other disorders.

- **Review of Educational and Occupational Histories**: Understanding the patient's academic and work experiences can provide valuable insights into how ADHD symptoms have manifested and impacted their life over time.

- **Psychological Testing**: In some cases, formal psychological testing can be beneficial to assess cognitive functioning, attention, memory, and other areas that might be affected by ADHD and co-occurring conditions.

- **Medical Examination**: A physical examination to rule out other medical conditions that could mimic or contribute to ADHD symptoms.

- **Collaboration with Other Professionals**: Engaging with educators, occupational therapists, or other healthcare providers can offer additional perspectives and information that aid in the diagnostic process.

It's also important for clinicians to consider the developmental aspects of ADHD and its symptoms across the lifespan. ADHD can manifest differently at different ages, and a comprehensive assessment should take into account the developmental stage of the individual.

ADHD Self-Assessment Test

This assessment test has been crafted solely for guidance and informational purposes. It is crucial to understand that this is not a diagnostic tool. This self-assessment is not intended to diagnose Attention Deficit/Hyperactivity Disorder (ADHD) nor should it be seen as a substitute for a professional evaluation.

Please be aware of its limitations: while this test may help identify potential symptoms of ADHD, its results are not definitive or conclusive. ADHD symptoms can be indicative of a variety of conditions, and this test cannot differentiate between them.

For an accurate diagnosis and a tailored treatment plan, it is essential to consult a healthcare professional. They are equipped to conduct a comprehensive assessment, considering that ADHD often shares symptoms with other conditions, and can provide the most appropriate guidance for your individual needs.

Instructions:

Rate each statement based on your experiences over the past six months.

Use the following scale for your responses:

- 0 = Never
- 1 = Rarely
- 2 = Sometimes
- 3 = Often
- 4 = Very Often

Test Statements:

1. I have difficulty sustaining attention in tasks or play activities. (0-4)

2. I often make careless mistakes in schoolwork, work, or

other activities. (0-4)

3. I struggle to follow through on instructions and fail to finish schoolwork, chores, or duties. (0-4)

4. I experience challenges in organizing tasks and activities. (0-4)

5. I avoid, dislike, or am reluctant to engage in tasks that require sustained mental effort. (0-4)

6. I often lose things necessary for tasks or activities (e.g., school materials, keys, paperwork). (0-4)

7. I am easily distracted by extraneous stimuli (e.g., unrelated thoughts or sounds). (0-4)

8. I am often forgetful in daily activities (e.g., doing errands, returning calls). (0-4)

9. I fidget with or tap hands or feet or squirm in my seat. (0-4)

10. I often leave my seat in situations when remaining seated is expected. (0-4)

11. I feel restless or act as if "driven by a motor." (0-4)

12. I often talk excessively. (0-4)

13. I blurt out answers before questions have been completed. (0-4)

14. I have difficulty waiting my turn. (0-4)

15. I interrupt or intrude on others (e.g., butt into conversations or games). (0-4)

Scoring:

- Add up the scores for each item to get a total score.

- The higher your score, the more symptoms you may have related to ADHD.

Score Interpretation:

- **0-20:** Indicates fewer ADHD-related symptoms. However, if you have concerns or if any symptoms are present, a professional assessment is still advised.

- **21-40:** Some ADHD-related symptoms are indicated. It is advisable to seek a professional assessment, especially if these symptoms are affecting your daily life.

- **41-60:** Indicates a moderate to high number of ADHD-related symptoms. A professional assessment is strongly recommended.

What to Do Next:

- Regardless of your score, if you have concerns about ADHD or related symptoms, it is important to consult with a healthcare professional. This self-assessment can serve as a starting point for discussion.

- Even a lower score does not rule out ADHD or other conditions, as individual experiences and symptoms can vary widely.

- Remember, this self-assessment is not a substitute for a professional diagnosis. Only a qualified healthcare professional can provide an accurate diagnosis and recommend appropriate treatment.

Highlights of The Chapter

ADHD in women presents a unique set of challenges that often go unnoticed due to common misconceptions and societal expectations. Unlike the well-known image of the hyperactive boy, women with ADHD are more likely to experience symptoms like difficulty focusing, disorganization, and emotional sensitivity. These symptoms can be subtle and are frequently overlooked or mistaken for other issues, leading to underdiagnosis or misdiagnosis.

Society tends to expect women to be naturally organized and emotionally stable, which only intensifies the pressure and challenges for those with ADHD. Adding to the complexity, hormonal changes throughout a woman's life, such as during puberty, menstruation, pregnancy, and menopause, can exacerbate ADHD symptoms, making management even more challenging.

The journey to a correct diagnosis for women with ADHD can be long and fraught with obstacles. Many encounter skepticism from healthcare professionals or are incorrectly diagnosed with conditions like anxiety or depression. This is compounded by the fact that ADHD often coexists with other mental health issues, making diagnosis and treatment even more complex.

Key Points:

- **Subtle Symptoms**: Women with ADHD often struggle with inattention and organization rather than hyperactivity, leading to challenges in daily life and work that can go unnoticed.

- **Societal Expectations**: The societal pressure on women to excel in multitasking and emotional regulation exacerbates the difficulties faced by those with ADHD, often leading to feelings of inadequacy.

- **Hormonal Influence**: Hormonal fluctuations can significantly impact ADHD symptoms in women, requiring a tailored approach to treatment and support.

- **Diagnosis Challenges**: Many women with ADHD experience delays in diagnosis or are misdiagnosed with other mental health conditions due to a lack of awareness about how ADHD manifests in females.

- **Comorbidity Complications**: ADHD in women frequently occurs alongside other conditions like anxiety and depression, adding layers to the diagnostic and treatment process.

- **Treatment Tailoring**: Effective management of ADHD in women requires an approach that considers the unique challenges they face, including societal pressures and hormonal changes.

- **Advocacy for Awareness**: Increasing awareness and understanding of ADHD in women is crucial to improving diagnosis, treatment, and support for those affected.

Chapter 3: Emotional Aspects of ADHD

Jumping straight in, this chapter tackles the essence of ADHD for women. It's not just about forgetfulness or daydreaming but digging into our identity in a world that often misreads our vibrant minds.

We're unraveling the identity enigma, showing how ADHD shapes our thoughts, connections, and self-view. Instead of seeing ADHD as a hurdle, we're celebrating its gifts, like creative genius and deep empathy.

Next, we face the emotional whirls of feeling like frauds or drowning in tasks. But, we're flipping the script with real talk and tools to smooth out those highs and lows.

We're also tackling daily hurdles, offering life hacks to slice through the chaos and keep our cool.

Then, there's the heavy duo of guilt and shame. We're dissecting why they hit so hard and how to shed that weight.

Feeling ultra-sensitive to rejection? We dive into why our brains ramp up these feelings and how to tone them down.

Consistency might as well be a foreign word with our ever-changing energy and focus, but we're learning to ride these waves with grace.

Socially, ADHD can be a maze, but we've got pointers to keep connections strong without burning out.

This chapter's about more than just coping with ADHD; it's about leveraging it to rediscover and empower ourselves. Let's get into it and emerge more tuned into making ADHD an asset, not an adversary.

Struggle for Identity

Navigating life with ADHD as a woman often feels like you're walking a tightrope between your true self and society's expectations. This journey goes beyond managing ADHD symptoms; it's about how ADHD colors your entire existence, affecting your thought processes, relationships, and how you fit into the world. Society's standards, which often prize organization, timeliness, and constant focus, don't always align with the experiences of someone with ADHD, leading to a sense of disconnection and self-reflection. Questions like "Who am I beyond my ADHD?" or "What could I achieve without these obstacles?" aren't just passing thoughts; they're deep dives into identity amid societal norms and personal dreams.

This search for identity can feel like a relentless challenge, prompting you to constantly evaluate your worth and capabilities against a backdrop of cultural ideals of success. Yet, adopting a new perspective on ADHD—as an integral part of your identity—can be liberating. Recognizing ADHD means acknowledging the unique strengths it brings, such as creativity, empathy, and the capacity for innovative thinking, alongside its challenges.

Embracing your neurodiversity involves a significant shift: viewing ADHD not as a set of problems to be fixed but as a core aspect of your being that enriches your perspective and abilities. It encourages a deeper self-understanding, compassion for your neurodivergent traits, and a celebration of the ways in which ADHD affects your interactions with the world.

The journey toward embracing your neurodiversity is marked by learning, self-discovery, and growing self-acceptance. It entails recognizing the impacts of ADHD on your life, identifying the positive aspects it brings, and understanding that your value extends beyond the difficulties. Embracing ADHD fully means moving beyond acceptance to a place of pride in your neurodivergent identity, honoring your unique needs, and advocating for environments where you can flourish.

Part of this process is building a supportive community that validates your experiences and shares insights, reminding you that you're not alone. It also means finding strategies that resonate with your ADHD brain, allowing you to navigate the world on your terms. Embracing your story with ADHD is about more than acknowledging a diagnosis; it's about integrating your experiences, challenges, and triumphs into your identity, viewing your journey through a lens of acceptance and strength.

Each person with ADHD has a distinct path, filled with its own hurdles and breakthroughs. Owning your narrative involves celebrating your neurodivergent differences, recognizing the value in your unique way of thinking, and leveraging your inherent strengths. This approach paves the way for a fulfilling life that reflects who you are, embracing the complexity of ADHD as a source of creativity, resilience, and profound personal growth.

Exercise: Rediscovering Your Identity and Values through ADHD

Part 1: Challenges and Growth

1. **What's Been Tough?**

   - Think about the hurdles you've encountered because of ADHD. Maybe it's keeping track of time, jumping on impulses, getting super absorbed in things you love, dealing with criticism, or keeping up with friends and family.

   - Reflect on how these challenges show up in different parts of your life, like at home, work, or when you're hanging out with people.

2. **Learning and Growing:**

   - Now, flip the script. How have these challenges helped you grow? Maybe they've made you appreciate the chaos, sparked your creativity, or taught you the power of bouncing back.

   - Jot down those aha moments or times when you overcame something tough, and what you learned from it.

Part 2: Values and Who You Are

1. **What Matters to You:**

- Based on everything you've thought about, what values stand out to you now? Has your ADHD journey made certain values more important, like being understanding, creative, or resilient?

- Share how ADHD has brought these values to life. For example, if understanding others is big for you, how has ADHD helped you get there?

2. **Your Identity:**

- How has ADHD shaped who you are? Think about the traits or parts of your identity that you see as linked to your ADHD experience.

- Write about how embracing ADHD has given you a fuller picture of yourself and your place in the world.

Part 3: Your Story

1. **Putting It All Together:**

- Time to weave your reflections into your own story. Start with the tough stuff and how it's shaped who you are and what you value.

- Highlight those moments of growth and acceptance. How have they brought you closer to understanding yourself and your ADHD?

2. **Looking Ahead:**

- Think about what accepting your ADHD means for your future. What dreams do you have, and how does your unique ADHD perspective help you chase them?

- Write about your hopes and how you see yourself moving forward, armed with your strengths and values.

Reflecting and Maybe Sharing:

- After you've written your story, take a step back. How does it feel to see your journey laid out? Has putting it into words changed how you see yourself or your ADHD?

- If you're feeling brave, think about sharing your story with someone. It can be a powerful way to connect, spread understanding, and fully embrace who you are.

This isn't just a task; it's a chance to throw a little party for yourself, to honor your adventure with ADHD, and to recognize all the incredible ways it's shaped the unique and amazing person you are. Diving into this exercise will do wonders for you, especially as you tackle Chapter 10. So, why wait? Jump into it right now and start celebrating you!

Impostor Syndrome

Ever felt like you're just faking it till you make it, and one day everyone's gonna figure out you're not as smart or capable as you seem? That's impostor syndrome in a nutshell. It hits a lot of us, but for women with ADHD, it's like that feeling is on steroids. Why? Because ADHD can make your performance all over the place. Some days, you're smashing it, ticking off tasks like there's no tomorrow. And then, out of nowhere, even the smallest stuff feels like climbing Everest. This rollercoaster can make any win feel more like a fluke than something you've earned through hard work and talent.

ADHD can throw you some real curveballs, messing with your focus, how you organize your life, and even how you handle your emotions. For women dealing with all this, trying to live up to what society or we ourselves expect can be a real grind. We put in the extra mile, come up with all these clever ways to keep our symptoms in check, and when we do manage to pull off something awesome, our brain goes, "Nah, you just got lucky or tricked everyone into thinking you're better than you are."

This whole deal sets off a nasty cycle of doubting ourselves and worrying that someday, someone's going to call us out. It's especially tough in places like work, where messing up isn't exactly celebrated. The fear of being outed as an impostor can stop us from going after promotions or even admitting to ourselves that, yeah, we did good.

So, what do we do about this impostor syndrome thing, especially when ADHD's part of the mix? First off, it's about realizing that this whole up-and-down with our achievements is just part of the ADHD gig. It doesn't mean we're not talented or worthy. Fighting these impostor vibes means bigging up our real wins, finding folks who get what we're going through (and won't judge), and being kind to ourselves. It's about seeing the ADHD challenges we face not as signs we're faking it but as hurdles we've managed to jump over.

Exercises: Challenging Impostor Thoughts

1. **Identify the Impostor Thought:**

    - When you notice a thought that suggests you're not good enough or a fraud, write it down. Be specific. For example, "I only got praise for my project because no one else knows how little effort I put in," or "I don't deserve to be in this position; I'm not as smart as they think."

2. **Question the Thought's Origin:**

- Reflect on where this thought is coming from. Is it based on facts, or is it a feeling? Write down your analysis. Often, impostor syndrome thoughts stem from feelings rather than factual evidence of your abilities or accomplishments.

3. **Gather Contradictory Evidence:**

- For every impostor thought, find evidence that contradicts it. This could be previous accomplishments, positive feedback from others, skills you've developed, or challenges you've overcome. If you're struggling, think about what a supportive friend might say about you. Document this evidence.

4. **Reframe the Thought:**

- Now, take the evidence you've gathered and use it to reframe the original impostor thought into a positive, affirming statement. For example, "I received praise for my project because I delivered quality work that met the project's goals," or "I deserve my position because I have the skills and knowledge needed, and I continue to learn and grow."

5. **Reflect on the Process:**

- After reframing your thought, reflect on how this process made you feel. Do you feel more confident? Less fraudulent? Recognize how challenging these thoughts can lead to a shift in your mindset over time.

6. **Repeat Regularly:**

- Impostor syndrome isn't overcome in a day. Make this exercise a regular practice, especially in moments of doubt. Over time, you'll build a stronger foundation of self-belief and reduce the frequency and intensity of impostor thoughts.

Tips for Success:

- Keep your journal or digital notes accessible for quick reflections.

- Be patient with yourself; changing thought patterns takes time.

- Celebrate small victories in changing your mindset.

This exercise is more than just a task; it's a step towards reclaiming your confidence and recognizing the value you bring, ADHD and all. By consistently challenging impostor thoughts, you're not only combating impostor syndrome but also building a more compassionate and accurate view of yourself.

Feeling Overwhelmed

Living with ADHD as a woman often feels like you're stuck in a never-ending storm of chaos and expectations. It's more than just trying to keep up with a never-ending to-do list or racing against time. It's about dealing with the pressure to be perfect in all the traditional roles society expects of women. From the moment you wake up, you're bombarded with a mental to-do list that doesn't quit—taking care of others, keeping your home spotless, being a star at work, and staying on top of your social life. The real challenge isn't just ticking off these tasks; it's the mental effort it takes to plan and juggle them all.

For women with ADHD, daily life feels like battling through a relentless storm where each task adds to the downpour of duties. Even simple things like making a doctor's appointment or tidying up feel overwhelming, leading to a cycle of stress and anxiety.

But there's a silver lining. Recognizing that feeling swamped is part of living with ADHD can be a game-changer. It doesn't mean you're not trying hard enough. Instead, it's a sign to adjust your approach. Breaking down big tasks into smaller pieces, finding a supportive community that understands, and adopting ADHD-friendly methods can help calm the chaos.

Changing how you define success can also relieve some pressure. Success isn't about having a perfect home or completing every task flawlessly. It's about focusing on what's truly important, appreciating the effort you've put in, and celebrating the small wins. It's crucial to remember that feeling overwhelmed isn't a permanent state, but a hurdle you can overcome.

Addressing the pervasive feeling of being overwhelmed requires a blend of practical strategies, self-compassion, and sometimes, a shift in perspective. For women with ADHD, finding effective ways to manage this sensation can transform daily life from a series of stressors to a more manageable—and even enjoyable—experience. Here are some practical approaches:

1. Break Tasks into Smaller Steps

This strategy is foundational. It directly addresses the common ADHD challenge of starting and completing tasks by making them more approachable and less daunting. Breaking tasks down helps overcome paralysis by analysis and the overwhelm that comes with looking at a big, undefined task.

- **Visualize the End Result**: Before breaking down the task, spend a moment visualizing what the completed task looks like. This can help clarify what sub-tasks are necessary.

- **Write Down Each Step**: Use a notebook or digital tool to list every step, no matter how small. For a project like preparing a presentation, steps might include choosing a topic, researching, outlining points, creating slides, and practicing the presentation.

- **Allocate Time Blocks**: Assign specific time blocks to work on each sub-task. For instance, dedicate 30 minutes to research, followed by a short break. Using a timer can help stay focused during these blocks.

- **Adjust as Needed**: Be flexible and adjust your sub-tasks or time allocations as you progress. Some tasks might take longer than expected, which is okay.

2. Use Tools and Technology

Leveraging tools and technology is essential for externalizing the mental load that contributes to feeling overwhelmed. Planners, apps, and reminders can compensate for memory challenges and attention issues, helping to manage time and tasks more effectively.

- **Digital Planners and Calendars**: Utilize digital

planners to outline your week or month. Google Calendar can be used to block out time for specific tasks, and apps like Trello or Asana can manage projects and to-do lists.

- **Reminder Apps**: Apps like Due or Todoist allow you to set reminders for both one-off tasks and recurring activities. You can set reminders for taking medication, meetings, or even to take breaks.

- **Voice Assistants**: Use voice assistants to add tasks to your to-do list or set reminders hands-free. This can be particularly useful when you're in the middle of something and don't want to stop to write something down.

3. Prioritize Tasks

Prioritizing tasks tackles the overwhelm from a strategic angle, ensuring that energy and focus are directed toward what truly matters or needs immediate attention. It helps in reducing the stress of having multiple tasks seem equally urgent, which is a common source of anxiety for individuals with ADHD.

- **Daily Top 3**: Each day, choose three high-priority tasks that need to be accomplished. This focus prevents the overwhelm that comes from a long to-do list and ensures progress on essential items.

- **The Eisenhower Matrix**: Draw a simple square, divide it into four quadrants, and label them as Urgent/Important, Important/Not Urgent, Urgent/Not Important, and Neither Urgent nor Important. Place your tasks in these quadrants to visualize where your focus should be.

- **Delegation and Boundaries**: Identify tasks that can be delegated to others or postponed. Setting boundaries by saying no to non-essential requests or delegating tasks can significantly reduce your load.

Guilt and Shame

Dealing with the whole guilt and shame thing when you've got ADHD, especially for us women, is like walking through a minefield. These feelings aren't just passing through; they set up shop and become part of the daily grind. Imagine carrying a backpack full of rocks labeled "should have," "could have," and "why didn't I?" That's pretty much the heavy load of guilt and shame many women with ADHD lug around.

Let's talk about where this guilt comes from. For women with ADHD, there's this huge gap between what society expects and the reality of living with ADHD. And it's not a tiny gap—it's like staring across a canyon. Trying to live up to the perfect image of being the best parent, top-notch professional, or ideal partner feels nearly impossible. The usual ADHD challenges, like keeping track of time, staying organized, or keeping focused, just make that gap feel even wider. We're going to dive into why guilt hits so hard, showing how ADHD makes it tough to meet even our own expectations, let alone everyone else's.

Then there's shame, which goes even deeper, attacking who you are at your core. It turns any slip-up or mistake into this big statement about not being good enough. This part is about shining a light on how nasty shame can be, growing from all those times you've felt misunderstood, judged, or like you've failed. Shame has this way of telling you that your struggles are because you're not trying hard enough, ignoring how hard it really is to deal with ADHD every day.

But it's not all doom and gloom. We're also going to look at ways to get through the stormy seas of guilt and shame. Realizing you're not alone in feeling this way because of ADHD can start loosening those feelings' hold on you. Seeing how unrealistic some of the standards we set for ourselves are (or the ones we think society expects of us) can help start lifting those heavy emotions off our shoulders.

There are strategies to tackle guilt and shame, and they involve looking at the problem from different angles:

Recognize the Source

- **Quick Check-In**: You know those moments when guilt or shame suddenly hit you like a wave? Maybe after forgetting an appointment or while struggling through a cluttered home? Take a deep breath. Pause. Gently ask yourself, "Is this heavy feeling because of my ADHD?" Recognizing this can feel like a soft lightbulb moment, illuminating the fact that it's not all on you; it's your unique brain wiring playing its part.

- **Reality Note**: Keep something handy for notes – could be a cute notebook that makes you smile or a simple app on your phone. When you catch yourself feeling down over something that went sideways, make a quick note of what happened and how it made you feel. You'll start to notice patterns, like maybe late afternoons are tough or certain tasks always trip you up. Spotting these patterns is like finding clues on a treasure map, leading you to better understand and manage those ADHD moments.

- **Adjust Your Lens**: Every morning, as you're sipping

your coffee or brushing your teeth, whisper to yourself, "My worth isn't defined by my ADHD." Think of it as putting on your mental armor for the day. It's a gentle but powerful reminder that you're so much more than the hurdles you face. Your unique brain has its quirks, sure, but it also comes with its own set of superpowers.

Challenge Unrealistic Standards

- **Standard Audit**: Grab a moment when you're feeling calm – maybe during a quiet morning or as you wind down at night. Write down three standards or expectations you've been holding yourself to that often end up making you feel guilty or ashamed. Try to keep it simple, like "Be on time for everything" or "Never forget any task."

- **Reality Check**: Look at your list and give each standard a quick check or X. Put a check next to the ones that genuinely matter to you, ones that resonate with your core values. Mark an X next to the ones that feel more like they're coming from outside pressure or that nagging voice of perfectionism. This step is about separating what truly matters to you from the noise of external expectations.

- **Goal Reset**: For any standard you marked with an X, let's do a little goal makeover. Rewrite it into something that feels more achievable and less pressure-packed. Instead of aiming for a spotless home, how about "Create one clean, calm space for myself"? It's about setting goals that are kinder and more aligned with the ebb and flow of living with ADHD.

- **Celebrate Small Wins**: At the end of each day, take a minute to reflect on something you accomplished that feels good. Maybe you managed to send off an important email, or perhaps you simply made your bed. Whatever it is, acknowledge it. These small victories are golden, and they deserve a moment in the spotlight. Celebrating them builds a bridge to self-compassion and chips away at those heavy feelings of guilt and shame.

Sensitivity to Rejection

Living with ADHD as a woman can sometimes feel like you're walking around with your emotional antenna cranked up way too high, especially when you're also dealing with Rejection Sensitive Dysphoria (RSD). Picture this: you're at work, and you send an idea via email to your team. Hours tick by with no response, and your mind starts racing. "Did I say something wrong? Do they think it's a stupid idea? Why did I even suggest it?" By the time someone finally replies with a simple "Great idea, thanks!" you've already gone through a rollercoaster of doubting your worth and feeling like an outsider. That's RSD for you. It turns the dial up on the usual worries about fitting in and being liked, making every little comment or side glance feel like a major disaster.

RSD isn't just about feeling extra sensitive to what people say or do; it's like your brain is set to react to rejection on a super intense level. For women with ADHD, this means that even a little criticism can feel like a personal attack, and the fear of rejection feels as bad as physical pain. We're going to dive into the science behind RSD to understand why those with it can find social stuff so tough and why those emotional reactions can be so strong.

When you're dealing with ADHD and RSD, trying to navigate social scenes can feel like you're lost in a maze filled with traps. Worries about what people think, reading too much into things, and stressing over potential rejection can make you want to avoid people altogether, which only makes feelings of loneliness and being misunderstood worse. We'll talk about ways to handle these social minefields, like how being clear in your communication, setting your own boundaries, and surrounding yourself with understanding people can make a world of difference.

Here's the thing: RSD can really mess with how you feel about yourself. Every time you think you're being rejected or criticized, it's like taking a sledgehammer to your self-esteem. You start to believe all those negative thoughts about yourself, which only makes you expect rejection more. We'll explore how RSD affects your self-image and share some strategies to help you build up a kinder, more realistic way of talking to yourself. It's about recognizing your strengths, challenging those automatic negative thoughts, and starting to see yourself in a more positive light.

Dealing with RSD, especially when you've got ADHD, means getting your arms around a whole bunch of stuff—understanding what's going on, being aware of how it affects you, and finding the right ways to handle it. We're aiming to not just give you tips on how to cope but also how to feel better about yourself and get through social situations without that constant fear of rejection. With the right support and some practical strategies, it's all about learning to manage these feelings so you can enjoy more confidence, stronger relationships, and a happier life overall. Let's work on turning down the volume on that emotional antenna and navigate the world with a bit more ease. Here are some straightforward and empathetic tips to help navigate the intense feelings associated with RSD, especially for women who might find their emotional antenna picking up every signal:

1. Ground Yourself in Facts

When emotions are high, and you're feeling overwhelmed by perceived rejection, grounding yourself in facts is a powerful tool. This technique helps break the cycle of negative thought spirals that are not based on actual events or responses.

- **How to Apply It**: As soon as you notice your mind racing with negative assumptions, take a deep breath and pause. Write down what triggered your feelings. Next, list the factual evidence you have that supports or contradicts your fears. For instance, if you're worried that a friend is mad at you because they haven't replied to a message, note down factual observations: "My friend mentioned being busy with work this week."

- **Making It a Habit**: Incorporate this fact-checking process into your daily routine. Whenever you feel doubts creeping in, gently remind yourself to look for the evidence. Keeping a dedicated journal for this practice can help make it a regular part of your coping toolkit.

2. Set Clear Communication Expectations

Miscommunications or delays in responses can be significant triggers for someone with RSD. Setting clear communication expectations upfront can minimize uncertainties and help manage anxiety related to waiting for responses.

- **How to Apply It**: Whenever you initiate communication that requires a response, be proactive in setting a timeline for when you'd appreciate feedback. This could be as straightforward as adding a sentence to your emails or messages, like, "Could you please share your feedback by end of day Thursday?" This approach not only helps manage your expectations but also clarifies the urgency or importance of the request for the recipient.

- **Benefits**: This strategy not only reduces your anxiety but also enhances your professional and personal relationships by fostering clear and respectful communication. It sets a tone of mutual understanding and respect for each other's time and responsibilities.

3. Visualize Positive Outcomes

Visualization is a powerful technique that can shift your mindset from expecting the worst to anticipating positive outcomes. This shift can significantly impact your emotional response in situations that might trigger your RSD.

- **How to Apply It**: Before entering a potentially triggering situation, take a few moments to close your eyes and breathe deeply. Picture a scenario where the outcome is positive. Imagine the details—how you feel, what you hear, and the reactions of others. For example, visualize sending your email and receiving a response that acknowledges your good idea with appreciation.

- **Making It Effective**: The key to effective visualization is consistency and emotion. Regularly practicing positive visualization can rewire your brain's reaction patterns, reducing the intensity of RSD over time. Additionally, try to genuinely feel the positive emotions associated with your visualization, as this emotional component reinforces the positive expectation.

By focusing on these three strategies and incorporating them into your coping mechanisms for RSD, you can create a more balanced emotional landscape. Grounding yourself in facts helps manage immediate reactions, setting clear communication expectations reduces uncertainty, and visualizing positive outcomes shifts your anticipatory emotions. Together, these strategies empower you to navigate social interactions and potential rejections with more confidence and less anxiety.

Challenges with Consistency

Keeping things consistent when you've got ADHD, especially for us women, feels like chasing a unicorn. It's not like we're just up and down with our willpower or motivation; this rollercoaster ride is wired into our brains thanks to ADHD. So, we're talking about trying to hit the same level of productivity every day, but instead, we're riding waves of super productive days and then hitting the brakes hard on days where even starting seems impossible.

Picture this: you're on a high, checking off every task on your list, feeling unstoppable. You go to bed thinking, "I've got this!" Then, the next morning, it's like someone swapped your brain overnight. You stare at your planner, but it's all just a blur of words. The energy and focus from yesterday are gone, and you're left wondering how to even start. This isn't about not trying; it's a frustrating hallmark of living with ADHD.

Ever notice how one day you're smashing through your to-do list, full of ideas and getting stuff done like a boss, and then, bam, you hit a wall? Suddenly, even the smallest task feels like you're being asked to climb Everest in flip-flops. We're going to dive into why our performance can flip-flop like this. There's a bunch going on here: maybe one day you're all in because the project's super interesting, but the next day you couldn't care less. Or maybe it's super quiet one day, which helps you focus, but then the next day, everything and everyone seems determined to distract you. And don't get me started on stress. It's like pouring gasoline on the ADHD fire, making it even harder to keep things steady. It's super important for us and the people around us to get that these ups and downs aren't about how hard we're trying or how skilled we are; it's just part of the ADHD package.

Dealing with this unpredictability isn't just a practical hassle; it hits hard emotionally, too. Imagine not knowing if you're going to be your best self or barely get by from one day to the next. It stirs up a mix of confusion, frustration, and sometimes even shame, especially when you're worried about living up to your own expectations or what others might be thinking. This emotional whirlwind can lead to anxiety and depression, making the consistency conundrum even trickier. We're going to look at ways to handle these feelings, like reminding ourselves to be kind and understanding to our own brains, and figuring out strategies to cope with the mental maze of ADHD.

1. Embrace Flexibility Over Perfection

The quest for perfection, especially for women with ADHD, can be an exhausting and often unattainable goal. Recognizing and accepting the natural variability in your energy and productivity levels is key. This doesn't mean lowering your standards but rather adapting them to work in harmony with your ADHD.

- **Practical Application**: Start each day with a quick self-check-in. Assess your energy and focus levels, and based on that, decide which tasks are feasible for that day. It's about working with your current state, not against it.

- **Adjusting Expectations**: If you have a high-energy day, use it to your advantage and tackle more challenging tasks or those requiring sustained focus. On lower energy days, shift your focus to tasks that are less demanding but still contribute to your overall goals.

- **Embracing Flexibility**: Develop a mindset that views flexibility as a strength. When plans change or tasks take longer than expected, remind yourself that adapting to these changes is a skill, not a failure.

2. Create a 'Can Do' List for Different Energy Levels

Having two separate to-do lists based on your energy levels can significantly reduce the pressure and overwhelm that comes with fluctuating productivity. This approach ensures you continue to make progress, tailored to how you feel.

- **High-Energy List**: Include tasks that require more focus, creativity, or decision-making. These could be work projects, planning sessions, or any activity that benefits from a higher level of engagement.

- **Low-Energy List**: Populate this list with tasks that are less demanding mentally or physically. This could include administrative tasks, organizing, or even self-care activities that don't require much mental effort but are still productive.

- **Implementation**: Keep these lists easily accessible and visible. Review and update them regularly to reflect your current priorities and tasks. This visual reminder can help you quickly choose tasks that align with your energy levels without the need to rethink your whole day.

3. Identify Your Productivity Patterns

Understanding your natural productivity rhythms can be a game-changer. By identifying when you're typically more energized or focused, you can align your tasks with these times, enhancing your efficiency and reducing frustration.

- **Tracking**: Use a journal or app to note your energy levels and productivity throughout the day. Include variables like time of day, type of task, and any external factors that might influence your productivity, such as diet, exercise, or sleep quality.

- **Analyzing Patterns**: After a few weeks, review your notes to identify any patterns. You might discover that you're more focused in the morning or that your energy dips after lunch.

- **Strategic Planning**: With this knowledge, strategically plan your tasks to coincide with these patterns. Schedule demanding tasks during your peak productivity times and save lower-energy tasks for when you know you'll be less focused.

By integrating these strategies into your daily routine, you create a more ADHD-friendly approach to productivity. Embracing flexibility, tailoring tasks to your energy levels, and aligning your work with your natural rhythms can help mitigate the inconsistency challenges posed by ADHD, leading to a more balanced and fulfilling daily experience.

Social Challenges

Hanging out and connecting with people should be fun, right? But when you're a woman with ADHD, it can feel more like you're trying to crack some secret social code. Instead of just chilling and enjoying the vibe, you're on the outside looking in, trying to figure out how to jump into conversations or keep up with everyone else who seems to get it.

Let's break down why mingling can be so tricky. For starters, ADHD can make it hard to catch all those little hints people drop or remember the details they shared last time you chatted, which might come off like you don't care. Then there's the whole impulsivity thing, where you might jump into the convo at warp speed or overshare, and suddenly, people are giving you the side-eye. And don't get me started on being late or forgetting you promised to meet someone. It's not that you're flaky or don't care; it's just another fun part of the ADHD rollercoaster that can make you seem a bit out of sync. With all the communication mix-ups ADHD throws your way, it's no wonder misunderstandings can pop up a lot. These aren't just one-off oops moments; they can really mess with your friendships and make it tough to build trust. But here's the deal: you can work through this by being super clear when you talk, fixing mix-ups ASAP, and letting people know where you're coming from. It's all about giving and getting a little grace and understanding that everyone's just trying to get by in this wild social world.

When you're worried about messing up or getting judged, it's tempting to just bow out of the social scene altogether. But while dodging the drama might feel good at first, it can lead you down a lonely path, leaving you feeling even more on the outside. This bit's about finding ways to step back into the mix, showing up as you are, and finding those spaces where you're welcomed with open arms—quirks and all. Building lasting friendships when you're juggling ADHD can seem daunting. But guess what? Your ADHD brain also comes with some pretty cool perks, like being super passionate about the things you love, thinking outside the box, and really getting people on a deep level. Here, we'll talk tips for playing to those strengths, like setting reminders so you don't flake out, and ways to keep the friend vibe going strong through the ups and downs.

Finding where you fit in is a big deal for everyone, but it's extra special when you've got ADHD. This part is your nudge to go out and find your people—the ones who get what it's like to live on ADHD time. Whether it's joining groups that share your interests or linking up with fellow ADHD warriors online, there's a whole world of folks who are ready to welcome you with open arms.

So, this is the lowdown on navigating the social seas with ADHD. It's about understanding the hurdles, yes, but also about embracing the journey towards finding your people and creating genuine connections. With a bit of self-awareness, some solid communication skills, and the courage to reach out, you can make friendships that not only last but also celebrate the unique person you are, ADHD and all. Here are some specific, easy-to-apply tips to help manage those social challenges and foster meaningful connections:

1. Use Reminders for Everything Social

- **Set alarms** on your phone for meeting times, when to leave the house, and even to check in with friends. This helps with punctuality and keeping promises.

2. Prepare Conversation Starters

- **Keep a small list** of general topics or questions in your phone notes. Glance at it before social gatherings to ease into conversations without stress.

3. Embrace the Power of the Pause

- **Take a breath** before jumping into conversations. This little pause helps manage impulsivity and gives you a moment to gauge the flow of discussion.

4. Follow-Up Notes

- After hanging out, **jot down key things** people shared with you in a note app. Refer back before the next meet-up to show you remember and care.

5. Schedule Regular Check-Ins

- **Pick a day each week** to send a text or call a friend. It keeps connections strong without overwhelming your schedule.

6. Choose Activities Over Coffee Chats

- Suggest doing an activity together instead of just hanging out. It could be a walk, a craft, or cooking. **Activities give structure** to socializing, making it less daunting.

7. Find Your Tribe Online

- Join online groups or forums related to your interests or ADHD. It's a low-pressure way to connect and share experiences.

8. Self-Compassion Reminder

- **Set a daily reminder** to think of one thing you did well socially. Shifting focus to positives can boost confidence over time.

9. Visualize Social Success

- Spend a few minutes **imagining a positive interaction** before it happens. It preps your brain for a good experience.

10. Acknowledge Your Efforts

- At the end of each day, **give yourself credit** for any social effort you made, big or small. Recognizing your efforts helps build confidence.

By incorporating these straightforward tips into your routine, you can navigate social situations more smoothly, making room for more joy and less stress in your social life.

Highlights of The Chapter

This chapter is all about diving into what it's like for women with ADHD and flipping the script on how we see it. Instead of just focusing on the tough parts, like being forgetful or feeling all over the place, it celebrates the cool sides too—like being super creative and really getting how others feel. It's packed with real talk on handling the emotional rollercoaster of feeling like a fraud, slicing through daily chaos with clever hacks, and ditching the heavy load of guilt and shame. Plus, it gets into the nitty-gritty of why rejection feels extra harsh and how to smooth out the ride. It's not just about coping; it's about making ADHD your superpower, understanding yourself better, and rocking your relationships without burning out. Here's the lowdown on turning ADHD into an asset, embracing your vibrant mind, and finding your groove in a world that doesn't always get it.

Key Points:

- **ADHD is More Than Distractions**: It's part of who you are, shaping your creativity, empathy, and how you see the world. Embrace it as a unique lens, not just a challenge.

- **Tackling the Emotional Ups and Downs**: Find tools and strategies to deal with feeling overwhelmed or doubting yourself. Remember, every win, big or small, is genuinely yours.

- **Life Hacks for the Win**: Cut through daily chaos with smart tricks and organization hacks that make life smoother and keep your cool.

- **Shake Off Guilt and Shame**: Dig into why these

feelings hit hard and how to lighten the load. Spoiler: It's about setting realistic standards and celebrating the small victories.

- **Dial Down Rejection Sensitivity**: Learn why rejection hits different and find ways to ease the sting, building up confidence in your social game.

- **Ride the Waves of Inconsistency**: Get that your energy and focus will ebb and flow. It's about flexing with the day, not beating yourself up for the slow ones.

- **Strengthening Social Ties**: Navigate social mazes with tips on clear communication and finding your tribe, making connections that truly understand and support you.

Chapter 4: ADHD in Daily Life

Ever felt like time's this wild, stretchy thing that just doesn't behave? Yeah, you're not alone. This chapter is all about exploring that wacky relationship between ADHD and how we experience time, especially when it comes to juggling work, personal life, and everything in between.

Time can be a real trickster when you have ADHD. One minute you're hyper-focused, and hours fly by like seconds. Then, there's the "time blindness" thing – when planning or keeping track of time feels like trying to catch smoke with your bare hands. Ever underestimated how long something will take and ended up in a frantic rush? That's what we're talking about.

Then there's our brain's now-or-never channel. If it's happening now, we're all in. If it's a future thing? Eh, not so much.

Plus, let's chat about dopamine – our brain's feel-good DJ that sometimes skimps on the beats, pushing us to seek those instant rewards.

But here's the cool part: we'll share some nifty strategies and tools to help make friends with time. Think visual timers, breaking tasks into baby steps, and setting up a cozy, organized space that actually works for us. It's all about understanding our unique brains, leveraging our strengths, and maybe even having a little fun along the way.

So, buckle up! We're about to unravel the mysteries of ADHD and time, turning those time management struggles into triumphs, and finding ways to make our environment a supportive sidekick in our everyday adventures. Let's do this!

Understanding ADHD and Time Perception

For a lot of us women with ADHD, understanding time feels like trying to navigate a foggy landscape without a map or compass. This chat's all about diving into that quirky dance between ADHD and how we see time, and how this plays out in everything from getting stuff done at work to keeping up with our personal lives.

Time's Weird Stretchiness

With ADHD, time doesn't play by the rules. It stretches and squishes in weird ways. Ever find yourself so deep into something you love that you look up and, whoops, where did the last three hours go? That's hyperfocus for you. But on the flip side, if something's dull as dishwater, a few minutes can feel like forever because your attention just nopes out. This stretchy time thing can be super confusing, making it tough to figure out how much time you really need for things and manage it properly.

The Whole "Time Blindness" Thing

"Time blindness" is a fancy way of saying that estimating how long stuff will take, sticking to schedules, and even just remembering the clock exists can be a struggle. It's not just about needing better organization; it's about how the ADHD brain processes time differently. You might constantly underestimate how long tasks will take, leading to a mad rush, delays, and the dreaded missed deadlines. It's not about not caring or not trying; it's just a part of how the ADHD brain ticks (or doesn't).

Now vs. Not Now

So, with ADHD, our brains are kinda like those old TVs that only have two channels: "Now" and "Not Now." If something's happening "Now," our brains are all over it like it's the season finale of our favorite show. But if it's on the "Not Now" channel, it might as well be static. Future tasks? They don't get airtime until they're banging on our door, demanding immediate attention. This black-and-white thinking makes planning ahead tough because our brains are tuned to the urgency of the moment, not the importance of what's down the road.

This isn't just about being scatterbrained or a last-minute Larry. It's about how our ADHD brains are wired. They're laser-focused on the present, which is great for dealing with immediate issues but not so hot when we're trying to juggle long-term projects or goals. The challenge here is tricking our brains into giving those future tasks some "Now" vibes, so we can handle them before they turn into last-minute fire drills.

Dopamine, Rewards, and the Clock

Now, let's talk about dopamine – our brain's own little hype man. Dopamine is all about that feel-good buzz we get when we achieve something, no matter how big or small. But here's the kicker: ADHD brains are a bit stingy with dopamine. This means we're constantly on the lookout for things that give us an instant dopamine hit. Think about it like craving a fast-food fix instead of waiting for a slow-cooked meal. It's quick, it's satisfying, and it's right there.

This quest for instant rewards makes us champs at chasing quick wins but kind of clumsy when it comes to long-haul goals. Those big dreams and projects? They're like slow-cookers. They promise a fantastic payoff, but our brains are too busy hunting for the microwave meals of gratification to notice. It's not that we lack ambition or determination; it's just that our dopamine-driven brains are hooked on the thrill of the immediate reward.

When Feelings Warp Time

Our emotions can also mess with how we experience time. Stressing about a deadline, feeling bummed about past time management oopsies, or getting super excited about something can all make our internal clock go haywire. This emotional side of time management adds another twist to the puzzle, making it even trickier to keep a steady pace.

Getting a grip on how we deal with time involves understanding these quirks and working with them, not against them. It's about setting up the right tools and tricks, like visual timers or clear schedules, and practicing mindfulness to stay in tune with the present. By getting real about how ADHD affects our sense of time, we can start to make peace with the clock, turning time from a constant battle into something we can actually get on our side. Here are some tools and habits designed to help navigate and enhance your relationship with time:

1. Visual Time Aids

- **Use Large, Visible Clocks**: Place big clocks in frequently used rooms to keep time in your immediate visual field.

- **Timers for Tasks**: Employ kitchen timers, phone timers, or timer apps to break work into manageable chunks. The Pomodoro Technique, which involves working for 25 minutes and then taking a 5-minute break, can be especially effective.

- **Color-Coded Calendars**: Utilize digital calendars with color coding for different types of tasks or appointments. This visual distinction helps in quickly assessing your day or week at a glance.

2. Break Tasks into Smaller Steps

- **Task Decomposition**: Break down larger tasks into smaller, actionable steps. This makes it easier to estimate how much time each part will take and reduces the overwhelm that can come with big projects.

3. Set Up Reminders and Alarms

- **Multiple Alarms**: For important deadlines or appointments, set several alarms at intervals leading up to the event. This provides incremental nudges and reduces the chance of time slipping away unnoticed.

- **Reminder Systems**: Use apps that allow for recurring reminders for daily routines or weekly tasks. Having a set time each day to review and set up your reminders for the next day can help keep you on track.

4. Create Time Cushions

- **Build in Extra Time**: When planning your day or estimating how long a task will take, add a "time cushion" to account for the unexpected. This helps mitigate the stress of underestimating task duration and allows for a more realistic approach to scheduling.

5. Implement Regular Check-ins

- **Midday Review**: Take a few minutes each day, perhaps after lunch, to review what you've accomplished and what's still ahead. This can help adjust your plan based on how the day is actually unfolding.

- **Evening Preview**: Spend a few minutes each evening looking at the next day's schedule. This helps prepare your mind for what's to come and can improve your time awareness.

6. Prioritize and Plan

- **Top Three Tasks**: Each morning, or the night before, decide on the top three tasks you want to accomplish. Focusing on these can help guide your day and ensure that you're spending time on what matters most to you.

- **Weekly Planning Session**: Dedicate time each week to plan out the major tasks and appointments for the coming week. This broader view helps in allocating time more effectively and can reduce the anxiety of the unknown.

7. Mindfulness and Time Awareness

- **Mindfulness Practices**: Engage in mindfulness exercises designed to enhance present-moment awareness. This can be especially helpful in managing the ADHD tendency to get lost in tasks (hyperfocus) or to avoid tasks (avoidance due to overwhelm).

- **Reflection**: Spend a few minutes at the end of each day reflecting on your time use. Consider what went well and what could be improved, not as a critique but as a learning process.

8. Seek Support and Accountability

- **Accountability Partner**: Pair up with a friend, colleague, or coach who can help you stay on track with your time management goals. Regular check-ins can provide motivation and accountability.

By incorporating these strategies, women with ADHD can develop a more harmonious relationship with time, transforming it from a source of stress into a resource that supports personal and professional growth. Remember, it's about progress, not perfection. Celebrate the small victories and keep adjusting strategies as you learn what works best for you.

Organizational Strategies for Home

For women with ADHD, the endeavor to maintain an organized home can often seem like an uphill battle, with the goal of a harmonious living space appearing just out of reach. However, the essence of organization for individuals with ADHD shouldn't hinge on achieving an immaculate environment but rather on crafting a space that fosters a sense of calm, clarity, and efficiency.

Diving into home organization isn't just about making things look pretty or finding the perfect spot for everything. It's about crafting a space that really works for us, especially when ADHD is in the mix. Imagine trying to solve a new puzzle every day. That's what it's like trying to keep on top of meal planning, cleaning, and all the schedules. Kicking off any task often needs a bit more than just the usual nudge, particularly when the finish line doesn't come with immediate high-fives. And staying focused? That's a whole adventure on its own, kind of like trying to grab hold of a fish that just won't stay still.

Now, shift gears to the work world, and you've got a whole different battle. The office setup, supposed to help keep us on track, can sometimes feel more like a straitjacket, squashing down on the creativity and flexibility we thrive on. Juggling deadlines, figuring out what needs to jump to the top of the list, and not freezing up over big projects add extra layers to the organizational puzzle.

Under all this is the invisible stuff—the brain power and emotional energy it takes to just get through the day with ADHD. It's about the endless strategizing, making up for missteps, and constantly recalibrating to hit our own marks and meet what's expected from us. All this mental juggling, from remembering what's next to dealing with the unexpected, can be downright draining.

Throw in family life and childcare, and the complexity level just skyrockets. Playing the roles of parent, partner, and sometimes caregiver while keeping that organizational plate spinning? It's like navigating through a maze blindfolded. Trying to manage everyone's schedules and needs, on top of our own, can sometimes feel like a Herculean task. And the emotional side of things doesn't get any easier, demanding a level of mental juggling that's tough to keep up with.

But here's the silver lining: amidst the chaos, our ADHD-driven creativity, flexibility, and resilience shine through, giving us unique strengths that truly make a difference in family life. This organizational journey is full of challenges, sure, but it's also packed with moments of triumph and ingenuity.Here are some strategic approaches to creating such a space:

Establishing Zones

Creating specific zones in your home can drastically improve its functionality and reduce decision fatigue. Here's how to refine this approach:

- **Work Zone Enhancement:**

- Choose a spot with natural lighting to boost mood and productivity.

- Invest in ergonomic furniture to ensure comfort during long work periods.

- Keep a small plant or motivational quotes in the area to enhance focus and inspiration.

- **Relaxation Zone Upgrades:**

  - Incorporate elements like a soft throw blanket, a small bookshelf with your favorite reads, or a Bluetooth speaker for calming music to make the space inviting.

  - If possible, designate this zone away from high-traffic areas to minimize interruptions.

- **Meal Prep Zone Optimization:**

  - Invest in clear containers for pantry items to quickly see what you have and what needs restocking.

  - Install under-cabinet lighting to brighten work areas and reduce shadows, making cooking tasks easier.

  - Consider a magnetic spice rack on the fridge or a

hanging pot rack for easy access to cooking essentials.

Utilizing Visual Reminders

Visual reminders are crucial for staying on track. Enhance their effectiveness with these tips:

- **Whiteboards:**

    - Use color-coded markers to categorize tasks: work, personal, errands, etc.

    - Allocate a specific day for a weekly overview, where you update and organize your upcoming tasks and appointments.

- **Sticky Notes:**

    - Create a sticky note wall or section where you place all your notes. This can be an artful way to keep tasks visible and prioritize them.

    - Use different colors for varying levels of urgency or categories (blue for work, yellow for personal, etc.).

- **Open Shelving:**

- Label shelves or use shelf dividers to maintain order and designate spaces for specific items.

- Decoratively display items you love to inspire a sense of joy and creativity in your space.

Regular Decluttering

Maintaining a clutter-free environment is vital for focus and calm. Here's how to deepen this practice:

- **Set a Decluttering Schedule:**

  - Break down your decluttering schedule by zones and tackle one zone at a time to avoid overwhelm.

  - Use a timer to work in short bursts, making the task less daunting and more manageable.

- **One-In, One-Out Rule:**

  - Take photos of items you're unsure about keeping. If you don't miss them after a month, donate or discard them.

  - Regularly review and declutter digital spaces as well, such as your email inbox and digital files, to reduce digital clutter.

- **Use Baskets and Bins:**

  - Label baskets and bins with their contents or intended use to avoid misplacing items.

  - Have a "miscellaneous" bin for items that don't have a home yet; sort through it during your regular decluttering sessions to assign things a proper place.

Implementing these enhanced organizational strategies can significantly impact the daily life of individuals with ADHD by reducing stress, improving focus, and creating a more enjoyable living environment.

Highlights of The Chapter

This chapter dives into the quirky relationship between women with ADHD and time management, shining a light on why time often feels like a frenemy. It breaks down the concept of "time blindness," where estimating tasks, sticking to schedules, and even just clock-watching can feel like a Herculean task. We explore the ADHD brain's live-in-the-moment approach, which tends to ignore anything not happening "Now," making future planning a bit of a puzzle. The role of dopamine in seeking immediate rewards over long-term gains gets a spotlight, showing why quick wins often outweigh distant goals. Plus, we tackle how emotions can twist our perception of time, adding another layer of complexity to managing it. The chapter wraps up with practical strategies to buddy up with time, like using visual aids, breaking tasks into bite-sized pieces, and setting up systems that turn our space into a supportive ally in the organizational chaos. It's all about understanding these ADHD quirks and working with them to craft a life that's organized, fulfilling, and in sync with our unique brains.

Key Points:

- **Understanding "Time Blindness"**: Recognize the ADHD challenge of grasping time and learn strategies to mitigate its impact on daily life.

- **"Now vs. Not Now" Perception**: Work on techniques to bring future tasks into the "Now" to improve planning and execution.

- **Dopamine's Role**: Acknowledge the search for instant gratification and find ways to balance short-term rewards with long-term goals.

- **Emotional Time Warp**: Be aware of how feelings influence time perception and use tools to maintain a balanced view.

- **Strategic Organizing**: Implement organizational strategies tailored to ADHD, focusing on creating functional and calming spaces.

- **Visual Aids and Reminders**: Utilize visual tools to keep track of time and tasks, aiding in better time management.

- **Declutter and Simplify**: Regularly declutter and organize your living and working spaces to reduce stress and improve focus.

Chapter 5: Financial Management with ADHD

Talking about ADHD often leads us down familiar paths—juggling schedules, trying to keep things organized, and figuring out how to play nice in social settings. But there's this whole other battlefield that doesn't get nearly enough airtime: managing our finances. For a lot of women with ADHD, dealing with money isn't just about making sure the numbers add up or stashing away cash for a not-so-sunny day. It's about dodging those impulse buys, sticking to a budget without getting bored or overwhelmed, and making plans that stretch further than next week—all things that can feel like climbing a mountain when your brain is wired for ADHD.

This chapter is all about unpacking that tricky relationship between ADHD and keeping a handle on our finances. We're diving into the real deal—why impulsivity, inconsistency, and planning for the future can feel like Herculean tasks. And it's not just about pointing out the hurdles; it's about sharing some real talk on how to leap over them.

ADHD and Money Management Challenges

When it comes to handling money, for women with ADHD, it's way more than just keeping the numbers straight. It's like navigating a maze where your ADHD traits play a huge role in how you deal with your finances. This whole money thing is layered with challenges that go way beyond simple budgeting. We're talking about the full spectrum of financial health and planning for the future, all while wrestling with the classic ADHD lineup: impulsivity, distraction, and sometimes getting so zoned in on one thing that everything else falls off the radar.

Impulse Buys and the ADHD Brain

Diving deeper into this whole impulsivity gig, it's really all about dopamine—a brain chemical that's pretty much like the internal version of social media likes. When you've got ADHD, your brain is on a constant lookout for something, anything, that pumps out that dopamine quick. It's like your brain's reward system is tuned to a different frequency, always scanning for that next hit of instant gratification.

Now, when you spot something you want, your brain lights up like a Christmas tree. That dopamine surge is powerful, making the act of buying feel incredibly rewarding in the moment. It's not just about the joy of getting something new; it's about how your brain is wired to appreciate and seek out these quick fixes of happiness. This setup makes waiting or saving up—where the payoff is delayed and the dopamine release isn't immediate—seem way less appealing.

This craving for immediate rewards can turn shopping into a go-to source for that dopamine rush, especially when other aspects of life might not be delivering those quick wins. It's not uncommon to find yourself in a loop, where impulse buying becomes a reflex action to fill that dopamine gap, even when you know deep down it's not the best move for your bank account.

The result? A cycle of impulse shopping that can hammer your finances and leave you wrestling with a mix of guilt and stress afterward. It's a tough cycle to break, especially when the immediate buzz of a purchase overshadows the long-term satisfaction of hitting financial goals.

When Paying Attention Pays Off

Then there's the challenge of staying focused on the mundane yet crucial bits of managing money, like keeping up with bills or tracking where your cash is going. Thanks to ADHD, sticking with these tasks can feel like trying to watch paint dry. This often boils down to the ADHD brain's approach to executive functions, like remembering stuff and planning ahead, which can make financial upkeep feel like navigating a minefield blindfolded. A game-changer here can be setting up automatic payments for your bills or using tools that make financial tracking less of a chore and more like a game.

Hyperfocus: A Double-Edged Sword

Hyperfocus can be awesome when it's on your side, like when you're so into a project that everything else fades away. But when it comes to managing your money, getting too wrapped up in other stuff can mean your finances get the cold shoulder. Finding a way to make financial tasks engaging or rewarding can help pull some of that hyperfocus back to where it's needed, turning a potential pitfall into a plus.

Building a Better Financial Blueprint

Getting a handle on how impulsivity, distraction, and hyperfocus affect your financial habits opens the door to strategies that really work for the ADHD brain. It's about leaning on tools, people, and practices that can help shore up those areas where ADHD makes financial management tough. And by getting to grips with why your brain might be steering you towards certain financial behaviors, you can start to approach money management with a bit more kindness and a lot more savvy, transforming challenges into opportunities to flex those financial muscles in a way that suits you best.

Budgeting and Financial Planning Strategies

Budgeting and financial planning are crucial skills, especially for individuals with ADHD, who might find managing finances particularly challenging due to difficulties with organization, impulsivity, and maintaining consistent habits. Here are some practical strategies to help simplify the budgeting and financial planning process:

1. Start with Clear Financial Goals

- **Define Your Objectives**: Whether it's saving for a vacation, building an emergency fund, or paying off debt, having clear, actionable goals can motivate you and give your budgeting efforts direction.

- **Small Steps**: Break down larger financial goals into smaller, manageable milestones. Celebrating small wins can boost your motivation and sense of accomplishment.

2. Use Budgeting Apps

- **Automate the Process**: Leverage technology to simplify budget tracking. Apps like Mint, YNAB (You Need A Budget), or PocketGuard can help you monitor spending, categorize expenses, and stay on top of bills with less effort.

- **Set Notifications**: Use app notifications for bill reminders, low balance warnings, or weekly spending summaries to stay informed and make adjustments in real-time.

3. Simplify Your Accounts

- **Consolidate Accounts**: Reduce the number of checking and savings accounts to streamline your finances and make them easier to manage.

- **Automate Savings**: Set up automatic transfers to your savings account right after payday. This "pay yourself first" approach ensures you're consistently saving without having to think about it each month.

4. Implement the Envelope System

- **Physical or Digital**: Use physical envelopes with cash

for different spending categories or a digital equivalent through budgeting apps. Once the money in an envelope is gone, that's it for spending in that category until the next budgeting period.

- **Visual Cues**: For physical envelopes, keeping them in a visible location can serve as a constant reminder of your budgeting goals and limits.

5. Plan for Impulse Spending

- **Set Aside Fun Money**: Allocate a specific amount of money each month for impulse buys or treats. This can help satisfy the urge to spend without derailing your budget.

- **Impulse Wait Period**: Implement a waiting period for non-essential purchases. If you still want the item after a week, for example, and it fits within your budget, then consider making the purchase.

6. Regular Financial Check-Ins

- **Weekly Reviews**: Set a regular time each week to review your budget, track spending, and adjust as necessary. This can help catch any issues early and keep you on track.

- **Monthly Planning Sessions**: Use the end of each month to evaluate your financial progress, adjust goals, and plan for the next month. Reflecting on what worked or didn't can help refine your strategy.

7. Educate Yourself

- **Financial Literacy**: Invest time in learning about personal finance, whether through books, podcasts, or online courses. Understanding the basics of saving, investing, and debt management can empower you to make informed decisions.

8. Seek Professional Advice

- **Financial Advisor**: If managing finances feels overwhelming, consider consulting with a financial advisor. They can offer personalized advice, help you develop a financial plan, and keep you accountable.

9. Create a Buffer

- **Emergency Fund**: Aim to build an emergency fund to cover unexpected expenses. Start small, even if it's just a little each month, until you've saved enough to cover at least three to six months of living expenses.

10. Celebrate Progress

- **Acknowledge Achievements**: Don't forget to celebrate when you reach a financial milestone. Recognizing your progress can reinforce positive financial habits and keep you motivated.

By implementing these strategies, individuals with ADHD can create a structured, manageable approach to budgeting and financial planning that accommodates their unique challenges and supports their financial well-being.

Overcoming Impulsive Spending

Cracking the code on why we sometimes go on those impulsive spending sprees, especially for us gals with ADHD, means peeling back the layers to see what's really going on beneath the surface. It's not just about that sudden urge to buy something cool or the rush we get from snagging a deal. There's a whole tangle of reasons tied up in the ADHD experience that makes impulse buying way more than just a fleeting lapse in judgment.

Riding the Emotional Rollercoaster

One big piece of the puzzle is how we handle our emotions. ADHD can make the emotional ride a bit more like a rollercoaster, with feelings swinging high and low super quickly. Sometimes, snagging something new is a quick fix to try and smooth out those highs and lows. It could be about lighting up a dull day with a bit of excitement or trying to push away the blues, loneliness, or just feeling totally overwhelmed. In those moments, buying something feels like it fills an emotional gap, even if it's just for a little while.

The Thrill of the New

Then there's our brain's constant lookout for something shiny and new. It's like we're on a never-ending quest for the next thing that'll give us a buzz. This can easily turn into a shopping habit, where each new purchase promises that kick of excitement we're craving. But the buzz doesn't last, and soon we're off seeking the next thrill, which can mean more spending and a cycle that's tough to break.

Who Am I, Anyway?

For some of us, impulsive buying is also tangled up with how we see ourselves. If we're wrestling with self-esteem or not feeling sure about who we are, shopping can feel like a way to shape our identity. Maybe it's about buying stuff that matches who we wanna be or that feels like it'll make us fit in or stand out. But this kind of identity shopping is like putting on a costume—it might make us feel good for a bit, but it doesn't really get to the heart of who we are.

Hyperfocus Hits the Wallet

Hyperfocus isn't just for getting into the zone with work or hobbies—it can lock onto shopping too. When something catches our full-on attention, it's like the rest of the world (and our budget) fades away. This can lead to buying stuff without really thinking about the bigger picture or how we'll feel about it later on.

The Social Media Effect

And we can't forget about the impact of social media and ads. They've got a sneaky way of making us feel like we're not quite measuring up and that maybe, just maybe, buying something will give us a boost. For those of us with ADHD, this pressure to keep up or fit in can make the urge to buy even stronger.

When we start to untangle all these threads, it's clear that impulsive spending for women with ADHD isn't just about the money. It's wrapped up in how we're feeling, how we see ourselves, and our hunt for excitement and identity. Getting a grip on it means looking beyond our wallets and addressing the emotional and psychological stuff that's driving those spending urges. Here are targeted strategies to help mitigate the impulse to spend and foster healthier spending habits:

1. Implement a 48-Hour Rule

- Before making any non-essential purchase, wait 48 hours. This cooling-off period allows time for the initial impulse to fade and for more rational consideration of whether the purchase is truly needed or just a momentary desire.

2. Use Cash for Discretionary Spending

- Withdraw a set amount of cash for your discretionary spending each week. Using physical cash makes you more aware of the amount you're spending compared to swiping a card and can help limit impulsive buys.

3. Limit Exposure to Temptations

- Unsubscribe from marketing emails and unfollow social media accounts that often tempt you to make unplanned purchases. Reducing exposure to these triggers can significantly cut down on impulse buying.

4. Set Specific Financial Goals

- Having a clear financial goal (saving for a vacation, paying off debt) can help prioritize your spending. Visual reminders of these goals, like a picture on your fridge or a goal tracker on your phone, can serve as daily motivation to save rather than spend impulsively.

5. Create a Budget That Includes Fun Money

- Allocate a specific amount in your budget for "fun money" or discretionary spending. This allows for some flexibility and enjoyment without derailing your overall financial plans. Knowing you have this allowance can reduce the urge to spend impulsively elsewhere.

These targeted strategies focus on creating a buffer between the impulse to spend and the act of spending itself, helping to manage the financial impulsivity that can accompany ADHD. By implementing these simple yet effective practices, you can gain greater control over your spending habits.

Highlights of The Chapter

Navigating finances with ADHD isn't just about crunching numbers; it's a complex dance of managing impulses, planning for the future, and staying on top of daily money tasks—all while your brain plays by its own set of rules. This chapter dives deep into why things like impulse buys, sticking to a budget, and saving for the rainy days feel extra challenging for women with ADHD. It's not just about the thrill of the purchase but also about how our brains seek out quick dopamine hits, how we cope with emotions, and how we see ourselves. Plus, there's the whole deal with hyperfocus and the constant bombardment of social media and ads nudging us to spend. But it's not all doom and gloom. By understanding the ADHD-money connection, we can tailor strategies to our unique brains, like setting up systems that make financial management less of a bore and more of a win. From embracing tech tools that track spending to creating budgets that actually fit our lives, there are ways to make peace with our finances. It's about turning financial management from a battleground into a place where we can flex our strengths, meet our goals, and maybe even have a little fun along the way.

Key Points:

- **Understand the ADHD-Dopamine-Money Connection**: Recognizing how ADHD impacts financial decisions, particularly through impulse spending for quick dopamine fixes, is crucial.

- **Embrace Technology for Budgeting and Tracking**: Utilize apps and tools designed to simplify budgeting and expense tracking, making it easier to stay on top of finances.

- **Tackle Impulse Buying Head-On**: Implement strategies like the 48-hour rule to curb impulse purchases, helping to break the cycle of instant gratification.

- **Set Clear Financial Goals**: Having specific, achievable financial goals can help focus spending and savings efforts, making financial planning more engaging.

- **Allocate "Fun Money"**: Include discretionary spending in your budget to satisfy the urge to spend without derailing overall financial health.

- **Educate and Seek Support**: Increasing financial literacy and seeking advice from financial professionals can empower decision-making and accountability.

- **Celebrate Financial Wins**: Acknowledging progress towards financial goals reinforces positive behaviors and motivates continued effort towards financial wellness.

Chapter 6: Nurturing Relationships with ADHD

Coming to love and relationships is like trying to learn a complicated dance routine, especially for women with ADHD. This chapter is about taking a closer look at how ADHD plays a big role in women's love lives, tackling the ups and downs, the little mix-ups, and the big moments of connection that make up a relationship. We'll go on a journey to see how ADHD is not just a solo journey, but something that really gets woven into the whole relationship vibe, affecting the way we talk, share feelings, and handle everyday things with our partners.

When you're a woman with ADHD, it's like your relationship is colored with all the quirks and qualities of ADHD. It's not just about you; it's about how those ADHD traits stretch out and touch every part of being with someone. This means everything from the way you chat with each other, to how you deal with emotions, to just getting through the day-to-day stuff together gets influenced by ADHD. Getting why this happens is super important for both people in the relationship. It lays down the groundwork for a ton of understanding, patience, and coming up with ways to make the relationship strong—not just getting through the tough times but really growing closer and more supportive because you get each other.

Core Challenges in Romantic Relationships

Managing romantic relationships with ADHD is indeed a rollercoaster, filled with ups, downs, and unexpected turns. Picture this: It's Friday night, and you're both curled up on the couch, trying to dive into one of those heart-to-heart conversations. You're eager to share your thoughts, but as you open your mouth, it's like your brain is running a marathon. Your thoughts are sprinting ahead, but the words come out in a jumbled mess. It's frustrating, feeling like you're in a dense fog, trying to communicate through a thick glass wall.

Then there's the emotional whirlwind. Imagine a simple, off-hand comment about forgetting to pick up milk turning into a full-blown argument. Your emotions rocket from zero to a hundred in a flash, and what started as a minor oversight becomes a testament to deeper issues. It's exhausting, riding these emotional waves, where a tiny spark can ignite a firestorm of feelings.

Dealing with daily tasks adds another layer of complexity. It's Monday morning, and you've both overslept. The kitchen is a mess, there's a pile of bills on the table, and you can't even find your keys. What should be a straightforward plan to tackle the day feels like assembling a puzzle with missing pieces. On good days, you're a team, tackling chores with efficiency. But on the days when ADHD takes the wheel, a simple to-do list feels like a mountain you're both too weary to climb.

Creating a deep connection is another challenge. You're at a cozy dinner, the ambiance is perfect, but your mind wanders off to a million other places. You catch yourself mid-conversation, realizing you've missed half of what your partner said. It's disheartening, battling these impulses that pull you away from the moments that matter most. You yearn to be fully present, to soak in the love and warmth, but your mind has its own agenda.

Decision-making can feel like being lost in a maze without a map. It's Saturday, and you're trying to decide on plans for the evening. The conversation spirals from dinner options to a debate on whether it's a Netflix night or time for a romantic outing. The indecision breeds tension, as what should be a simple choice feels like a high-stakes negotiation.

Your affection and attention are as unpredictable as the weather. One day, you're showering your partner with love, planning surprises, and sending sweet messages. The next, you're distant, caught up in your own world, forgetting those small gestures that keep the spark alive. This ebb and flow leaves your partner puzzled, trying to decipher the signals and understand where they stand.

Social gatherings bring their own set of challenges. You're at a party, surrounded by friends and acquaintances. While your partner is effortlessly mingling, you're mentally rehearsing names and conversation starters, praying you don't blurt out something awkward. The effort to appear engaged is draining, turning what should be a fun evening into a nerve-wracking performance.

Time management, or the lack thereof, casts a shadow over shared moments. Birthdays, anniversaries, or simply being on time for dinner plans become sources of stress. Despite your best intentions, time slips through your fingers like sand, and the realization hits too late. It's not about not caring; it's about grappling with a sense of time that seems to operate on a different frequency.

Each of these added challenges underscores the complexity of navigating romantic relationships with ADHD. They highlight the need for patience, understanding, and open communication between partners. By acknowledging and addressing these hurdles, couples can work towards building a stronger, more resilient bond that not only withstands the storms but also cherishes the sunshine that comes after.

The Silver Linings: Harnessing ADHD Superpowers in Love

But hey, let's flip the script for a moment. Sure, managing romantic relationships with ADHD is a bit like trying to dance on a moving surfboard. Yet, what if I told you that very same surfboard is waxed with some pretty rad qualities unique to ADHD? That's right. Amidst the chaos, there lie hidden superpowers—creativity, out-of-the-box thinking, and a fiery passion—that can turn the ordinary into the extraordinary in romantic relationships.

Unleashing Creativity in Love

First up, let's talk creativity. Women with ADHD have this magical ability to think in colors outside the conventional palette. This means date nights are never boring, surprises are genuinely surprising, and the mundane? Well, it gets a makeover into something memorable. Imagine planning a simple dinner date, and instead of the usual dine-and-dash, you end up on a moonlit picnic under a blanket of stars, with a playlist that's just perfect. That's the ADHD creativity at work, transforming the everyday into adventures.

Thinking Outside the Relationship Box

Then there's our knack for out-of-the-box thinking. Women with ADHD aren't fans of the beaten path; they're trailblazers who prefer to carve out their own routes. This trait brings a freshness to relationships, where problem-solving becomes an exercise in innovation rather than frustration. Stuck in a rut? Not for long. With a perspective that sees solutions where others see dead ends, women with ADHD can navigate relationship challenges in ways that surprise and delight, ensuring the journey together is anything but predictable.

Passion That Burns Bright

And oh, the passion. If there's one thing that's not in short supply, it's the depth and intensity of passion that women with ADHD bring to their relationships. This isn't just about romantic gestures (though we've got those in spades); it's about the whole-hearted, all-in commitment to making things work, to loving fiercely, and to feeling deeply. Yes, this passion can make for a rollercoaster ride of emotions, but it's also the glue that binds, the spark that reignites, and the force that drives a relationship forward through thick and thin.

Embracing the Journey Together

So, while ADHD can indeed make romantic relationships feel like navigating a ship through a storm, it also comes with a set of unique strengths that can enrich and deepen these connections. It's about using our creativity to keep the flames of romance burning bright, employing our out-of-the-box thinking to tackle challenges together, and channeling our passion to show up for each other, every single day. Harnessing the unique aspects of ADHD can indeed transform the dynamics of romantic relationships, turning potential challenges into opportunities for deepening intimacy and connection. Here are some tips for women with ADHD to leverage their distinctive traits in love:

1. Channel Your Creativity into Thoughtful Gestures

Imagine planning an evening where every detail reflects something meaningful about your relationship. It could start with a homemade dinner, featuring dishes that hold special memories or inside jokes. Perhaps follow this with a custom scavenger hunt around your home or neighborhood, with each clue leading to a reason why you love them or a happy memory you've shared. The night could end under a makeshift fort in your living room, decked out with fairy lights, cozy pillows, and a movie that has significance to you both. It's these personalized, creative touches that turn a simple night into an unforgettable experience.

2. Leverage Out-of-the-Box Thinking for Problem Solving

When confronted with a challenge, such as feeling disconnected due to busy schedules, suggest an unconventional solution. For example, create a shared digital journal where you both write one thing you appreciated about each other or a fun moment from your day. You could even set a weekly "mystery date" where you alternate planning surprise outings or activities for each other without disclosure until the moment arrives. This approach not only addresses the issue at hand but injects excitement and anticipation into your relationship.

3. Embrace and Share Your Passion

Let your deep capacity for passion enrich your relationship by sharing what moves you. If you're passionate about a cause, involve your partner in a volunteer day that supports it, allowing them to experience firsthand what fuels your fire. Or, if there's a hobby that captivates you, plan a day where you introduce your partner to it, whether it's an art class, a hiking trip, or a music festival. Sharing these parts of your life opens up new avenues for connection and understanding between you two.

4. Communicate Openly About Your ADHD

Create a cozy, intimate setting for open conversations about how ADHD affects your relationship dynamics. Use this time to share your experiences, challenges, and how certain behaviors might be misunderstood. Prepare some specific examples to help illustrate your points, like recounting a time when impulsivity may have come off as thoughtlessness, explaining your feelings and thought process throughout. This heartfelt exchange can deepen your bond by building a foundation of empathy and understanding.

5. Plan Together, Enjoying the Process

Turn planning into a playful, collaborative activity. Set aside an evening with snacks and music to brainstorm and map out a dream vacation or a home improvement project. Use colorful post-its to jot down ideas, categorize them, and then arrange them on a large sheet of paper or a corkboard. This visual and interactive method of planning can make the process enjoyable and engaging for both of you, transforming it from a mundane task into a fun project.

6. Focus on the Present

Plan a "Here and Now" day. Start with a morning without phones, simply enjoying coffee together while sharing stories or dreams. Then, engage in an activity that's new to both of you, like taking a dance class together or exploring a part of town you've never visited. Throughout the day, encourage each other to notice small details—the taste of your lunch, the sounds of the city or nature, the feel of your hands holding. This practice of mindfulness can make you appreciate each other and the moments you share more deeply, fostering a closer connection.

7. Seek New Experiences Together

Transform your quest for novelty into shared adventures. Plan a monthly "mystery adventure" where you take turns organizing an unexpected day out or a new activity. It could be anything from a hot air balloon ride to a pottery-making class. The key is not to disclose the plan until the day arrives. This builds anticipation and excitement, making each experience a thrilling discovery for both. Sharing these new experiences can deepen your bond and create lasting memories.

8. Cultivate Patience and Understanding

Designate a "patience pact" evening. Light some candles, play some soft music, and take turns discussing moments when you felt misunderstood or needed patience from the other. Use a "talking stick" — whoever holds it has the floor to speak without interruption. This ritual can help both partners practice listening, empathy, and patience. Understanding that ADHD can sometimes lead to communication mishaps or forgotten tasks, this pact reinforces the commitment to support each other through misunderstandings with kindness and patience.

9. Celebrate Small Victories Together

Create a "victory jar" where you both write down small wins or sweet gestures from the other person on slips of paper, folding them and adding them to the jar. It could be as simple as making the bed, a thoughtful compliment, or a successful day of managing tasks. Once a month, open the jar and read the victories together. This ritual not only encourages you to acknowledge and appreciate each other's efforts but also serves as a reminder of your strengths and the positive aspects of your relationship.

10. Support Each Other's Growth

Embark on a "growth project" together. Choose something new you both want to learn or improve on, whether it's a language, a musical instrument, or fitness goals. Set aside regular times each week to work on this project together, supporting and encouraging each other's progress. Celebrate milestones with small rewards or recognition. This shared journey of learning and growth can strengthen your relationship, providing a sense of shared purpose and mutual support.

By weaving these strategies into the fabric of your relationship, you not only navigate the ADHD-related challenges more effectively but also enrich your partnership with deeper understanding, shared joy, and mutual growth. These actions highlight the strengths ADHD can bring to love, transforming potential obstacles into opportunities for building a more intimate and resilient bond.

Finding Balance: ADHD Women Facing Love, Parenting, and Expectations

Stepping into the world as a woman, especially when you're playing the dual roles of partner and parent, comes with a heavy load of expectations. Throw ADHD into the mix, and the challenge cranks up a notch. You're not just aiming to tick off society's checklist for being the ideal partner or parent; you're also wrestling with ADHD symptoms that can make the usual juggle feel like a circus act. The quest for perfection—in managing a home, nurturing relationships, and keeping everything running smoothly—can feel like an uphill battle in a world that doesn't always get the extra hurdles ADHD throws your way.

Imagine society's idea of success in love and parenting as a picture-perfect postcard, where every second is flawlessly divided between your partner and your kids, leaving no room for the messy realities of life. For those with ADHD, trying to live up to this image can feel like trying to force a square peg into a round hole. The unique way the ADHD brain is wired—with its special set of strengths and quirks—doesn't always gel with the expected norms of being on the ball 24/7, punctuality, and keeping emotions on an even keel.

It's not just about the struggle to stay focused, manage your time, or keep your emotions in check; it's also about the inner turmoil that comes from trying to match up to these societal standards. Distractions can make those precious moments with your partner seem scattered, emotional ups and downs can shake up the family peace, and the ADHD twist on time can turn planning and prioritizing into a minefield.

The world often rolls with a one-size-fits-all approach, sidelining the unique experiences of those with ADHD. The myth of the superparent or superpartner, effortlessly juggling every ball, sets a bar that's sky-high. This ideal overlooks the extra mile women with ADHD go every day, where even "simple" tasks can be a marathon of mental and emotional effort.

The key? Carving out your own path, one that celebrates your ADHD for what it is—a part of you, complete with its challenges and strengths. It's about trading the pursuit of perfection for self-kindness, acknowledging that chasing an impossible standard is a road to nowhere. Celebrate the wins, no matter how small, and lean into your unique abilities, whether it's out-of-the-box thinking, a knack for problem-solving, or the power of hyperfocus when it clicks.

Finding your tribe is vital, too. Connecting with folks who get it, who've walked in your shoes, can be a game-changer, offering a sense of community and understanding that's hard to find elsewhere. Seeking out professional advice, from therapists to ADHD coaches or support groups, can arm you with strategies tailored to making relationships and parenting work on your terms. These supports validate your experiences and help chip away at the pressure to conform to the norm.

For women with ADHD, it's all about rewriting the script—shaping a life that fits you, not squeezing into a mold set by societal norms. It's a journey of embracing who you are, finding acceptance, and adapting in a way that brings out the best in your relationships and family life. It's about living authentically, ADHD and all, and finding joy in the perfectly imperfect balance of love, parenting, and self. The balancing act of loving and parenting with ADHD doesn't come with a manual, but here are some real, down-to-earth tips that can make the journey a little smoother:

1. Dump the Superhero Cape

Imagine literally taking off a superhero cape and throwing it in the laundry basket. Now, breathe out. Accept that some days you're the maestro of multitasking, and other days, it's a win if everyone's fed and safe. This isn't a superhero gig; it's real life, complete with mess-ups and mismatched socks. Celebrate the perfectly imperfect you.

2. Teamwork Makes the Dream Work

Picture a tag team where you and your partner pass the baton back and forth, playing to each other's strengths. Maybe you're the queen of spontaneous fun, turning a dull afternoon into an impromptu indoor picnic, while your partner ensures homework and chores are done. Embrace this dynamic duo approach, where balance isn't about doing it all but doing what you do best together.

3. Scheduled Solo Time

Visualize a sanctuary space, a nook in your home that's just yours for a slice of the day. Whether it's a corner with a comfy chair and your favorite books or headphones at the ready for a music escape, guard this time religiously. It's the pause button you need to be your best self for everyone else.

4. Family Calendar Central

Think of your family calendar as mission control. It's a large, colorful command center where everyone's activities, from soccer practice to date nights, are in plain sight. Use stickers, markers, or whatever makes it fun and engaging. This isn't just about keeping track; it's about turning family logistics into a visual and collaborative art project.

5. Embrace Shortcuts

Shortcut strategies are your secret weapons. Picture a Sunday afternoon kitchen dance party while you batch-cook meals for the week or setting up birthday reminders that ensure you never miss sending a card. These hacks aren't just about saving time; they're about crafting pockets of ease in your daily hustle.

6. Connect with Your Tribe

Imagine a virtual or real-life living room filled with fellow ADHD warriors, where stories, struggles, and triumphs are shared over coffee or online chats. This tribe gets it, no explanation needed. It's a place where your ADHD moments are met with nods, not judgment. Finding your tribe means surrounding yourself with understanding and support that uplifts you.

7. Celebrate the Wins

Every small victory is a cause for celebration. Picture a family victory dance in the living room for those moments when everyone's shoes find the shoe rack or the dishwasher is unloaded without a prompt. These celebrations are reminders of the joy in the journey, not just the destination.

8. Routine Check-ins

Envision regular family huddles that feel more like team pep talks than formal meetings. It's a chance to check the emotional pulse of your family, share laughs, and address any snags before they unravel. These check-ins are the glue that keeps everyone connected and moving forward together.

9. Laugh It Off

Keep a mental blooper reel of those ADHD moments. Missed an appointment? Accidentally dyed the laundry pink? Instead of spiraling into frustration, share the story at dinner for a family laugh. It's about finding humor in the hiccups, reminding everyone that it's okay to be human.

10. Seek Professional Insight

Picture arming yourself with an arsenal of strategies, not weapons. This might mean bookmarking an article with tips for ADHD parents, joining a webinar, or attending therapy sessions. Seeking help is akin to downloading the latest software to upgrade your system – it's smart, proactive, and ultimately empowering.

Balancing love and parenting with ADHD is an art form, not a science. It's about painting outside the lines, turning the volume up on life's soundtrack, and dancing through the chaos with grace, humor, and a whole lot of love. Your family treasures the real, authentic you, ADHD quirks and all, forming a masterpiece of shared moments and memories.

Highlights of The Chapter

Navigating love and relationships with ADHD is like learning a complex dance, filled with unexpected steps and rhythms. This chapter explores how ADHD intricately weaves into women's romantic lives, affecting communication, emotional management, daily responsibilities, and the ability to connect deeply. It acknowledges the hurdles, from jumbled conversations and emotional whirlwinds to the challenges of daily tasks and decision-making. Yet, it also highlights the unique strengths that ADHD brings to love, such as creativity, innovative problem-solving, and intense passion. By understanding these dynamics, both partners can cultivate patience, open communication, and strategies that strengthen their bond. Embracing ADHD in relationships isn't about overcoming a challenge; it's about leveraging unique qualities to enrich and deepen connections, transforming potential obstacles into opportunities for growth and understanding.

Key Points:

- **Acknowledge ADHD's Impact**: Recognizing how ADHD traits influence relationship dynamics is crucial for both partners, laying a foundation for empathy and patience.

- **Communicate Openly**: Encourage honest and clear communication about ADHD's effects, fostering a deeper understanding and stronger connection.

- **Leverage ADHD Strengths**: Utilize ADHD's inherent creativity, passion, and out-of-the-box thinking to enhance the relationship, bringing freshness and excitement to everyday moments.

- **Adapt Relationship Strategies**: Implement practical strategies that play to the strengths of ADHD, such as visual reminders for important dates or creating engaging ways to tackle daily tasks together.

- **Cultivate Patience and Support**: Both partners should practice patience and offer support, recognizing that ADHD can make certain aspects of relationships more challenging but also more rewarding.

- **Seek Professional Guidance**: Consider seeking advice from therapists or counselors who specialize in ADHD to develop coping strategies and strengthen the relationship.

- **Celebrate the Unique Bond**: Embrace the unique connection that comes from navigating ADHD together, recognizing the growth, understanding, and deepened intimacy it can bring to the relationship.

Chapter 7: Workplace Challenges and Strategies

Working with ADHD, especially as a woman, throws us into a whirlwind of unique professional challenges. It's not just about handling our core job responsibilities; it's about wrangling a whole zoo of distractible monkeys tossed in by our ADHD. These obstacles impact everything from our daily tasks to our career paths, often leaving us juggling satisfaction and struggle in equal measure. It's a constant dance, trying to harmonize with the rhythm of ADHD as we navigate the workplace jungle.

Take those dreaded meetings, for example. They can stretch into eternity, feeling like an endless loop of chatter. Maintaining focus on the conversation without wandering off to dream about holiday getaways or lunch plans? A serious battle. And chiming in at the perfect moment? That's a delicate waltz in itself, leaving you yearning for a fast-forward button. Staying tuned in without succumbing to brain fog can be exhausting, transforming what should be a straightforward exchange into something draining.

Time management? It's less like planning and more like playing a guessing game where you're perpetually second-guessing yourself. How long will this actually take? What should I tackle first? It feels like we're eternally playing catch-up, scrambling to stay afloat instead of ever feeling ahead of the curve.

Focus? It's a capricious beast. Sometimes, you're hyper-focused, laser-beam intensity allowing you to block out the entire world while cranking out work. But this double-edged sword means neglecting other tasks, creating an imbalance in your work ecosystem. Then there's the flip side: mustering the energy to start less exciting tasks feels like trying to ignite a wet match – hello, procrastination city and a towering to-do list.

The social maze of the workplace adds another layer of complexity. Making small talk or deciphering the unspoken rules of office politics can feel like you're constantly playing detective. It's as if everyone else received a secret handbook on navigating work relationships, while you're left winging it, making it an uphill climb to truly feel like you belong.

And feedback? A whole other beast altogether. While intended to be helpful, it can sometimes land like a gut punch, making it difficult not to take it personally. Separating "work you" from "real you" during these chats feels like trying to untangle headphones that have been knotted in your bag – stressful and emotionally taxing.

So yeah, wading through the work world with ADHD is like navigating a jungle without a map. It's not just about doing the job; it's about managing all these ADHD quirks while trying to find solid ground in the workplace.

Advocating for Accommodations and Support

Feeling the need to adjust your work environment due to ADHD? It's not about simply "getting by," but about **unlocking your full potential** and achieving ambitious goals. The first step is **understanding how ADHD manifests in your work** and identifying specific changes that could make a significant impact.

Know Your Needs: Before speaking with HR or your manager, **clearly identify** the challenges you face and **specific adjustments** that could help. Maybe it's a quiet workspace for focused work, flexible hours to align with your peak productivity, or visual reminders for project management. Understanding your unique needs empowers a clearer conversation.

Frame it as a Collaboration: Shift the focus from "need" to "opportunity." Explain how these accommodations benefit not just you, but also the team or company. Highlight potential outcomes like **increased productivity, fewer errors, and improved collaboration**. Position it as a win-win situation.

Offer Solutions, Not Just Problems: Don't just present challenges; **propose actionable solutions**. Research and suggest specific tools, technologies, or adjustments that address your needs. This demonstrates initiative and makes it easier for your manager to implement changes.

Start Small, Start Smart: If there's initial hesitation, suggest a **trial period** for your proposed accommodations. This allows everyone to assess the impact and make adjustments as needed. It showcases your willingness to collaborate and minimizes disruption.

Document Everything: Keep a record of conversations and agreements, either through email or notes. This helps track progress, clarifies expectations, and provides a reference point for future adjustments.

Remember, You're Not Alone: Seeking support is crucial. Consider talking to a professional familiar with workplace rights or an ADHD coach who can guide you through the process. Having someone in your corner can boost your confidence and provide valuable guidance.

By taking these steps with **preparation, positivity, and a collaborative spirit**, you can advocate for the accommodations you need to thrive in your workplace. Remember, you're a valuable asset, and setting yourself up for success benefits everyone. Here's how to advocate for **supportive adjustments** that unlock your potential:

1. **Chart Your Success Path:** Self-awareness is key. Track your workday for a couple of weeks, noting your energy levels, peak productivity times, and tasks that trigger challenges. This data isn't just self-discovery; it's **concrete evidence** supporting your need for adjustments.

2. **Frame it as a Power-Up:** Don't frame your request as a favor. Begin by expressing your **commitment to excellence** and highlight how specific adjustments align with your strengths. For example, "I thrive in quiet spaces for deep thinking. Having a dedicated space could significantly boost my contribution to key projects."

3. **Find Your Work Champion:** Navigating accommodations can feel daunting. Consider connecting with a

mentor or advocate who understands ADHD. They can offer guidance, moral support, and even champion your needs, making your request more impactful.

4. **Focus on Collaborative Solutions:** Frame your requests as **mutually beneficial solutions**. For example, suggest working remotely on specific tasks to minimize distractions and maximize focus, ultimately leading to **improved project outcomes**. Remember, what benefits you strengthens the team.

5. **Embrace Open Communication:** Be prepared for a conversation. Your manager might have questions or counter-proposals. Listen actively, **explain the value** your suggestions bring, and be open to **collaborative solutions** that fit the team's workflow and goals.

Productivity Techniques and Focus Strategies

We now proceed with 8 powerful techniques and strategies specifically designed to help individuals with ADHD achieve their career goals and thrive in the workplace:

1. Leverage Technology for Mind Mapping

- **Mind Mapping Tools**: Adopt mind mapping software like XMind or MindMeister for planning projects and tasks. Mind mapping can visually organize thoughts and ideas, making it easier for individuals with ADHD to see connections and develop plans for complex tasks without feeling overwhelmed.

2. Utilize Audio Assistants for Reminders

- **Voice-Activated Reminders**: Utilize voice-activated systems like Google Assistant, Siri, or Amazon Alexa for setting reminders and alarms. Speaking out your tasks and having a verbal reminder can be more engaging and less likely to be overlooked than traditional notification methods.

3. Adaptive Work Scheduling

- **Flexible Work Blocks**: Instead of rigid time blocks, experiment with flexible work periods that align with your natural attention cycles. Recognize when you are most alert and productive and schedule your most demanding tasks for these times, allowing for shorter or longer work periods based on your current focus level.

4. Personalized Reward Systems

- **Immediate Rewards for Task Completion**: Create

a reward system that provides immediate positive reinforcement for completing tasks or meeting goals. This could range from a small treat to a short break doing an activity you enjoy, leveraging the ADHD brain's need for instant gratification to boost productivity.

5. Environmental Modifications

- **Dynamic Workspaces**: Change your workspace layout or location based on the task at hand. For tasks requiring deep focus, choose a minimalist setup with minimal distractions. For more creative tasks, a vibrant and stimulating environment might be more beneficial.

6. Strategic Email and Communication Management

- **Email Sorting Tools**: Use email management tools and techniques, such as sorting emails into folders or using apps that prioritize emails by importance, to reduce the overwhelm of constant communication. Schedule specific times to check emails, allowing you to maintain focus on tasks without constant interruption.

7. Utilize Transition Rituals

- **Transition Rituals Between Tasks**: Implement short rituals to help transition between different types of tasks or work modes. This could be a physical activity, like stretching or a short walk, or a mental exercise, such as a 2-minute meditation to clear your mind and refocus.

8. Social and Professional Support Networks

- **Join or Create ADHD-Friendly Workgroups**: Engage with or establish a support network or workgroup for individuals with ADHD. Sharing experiences, challenges, and strategies can provide valuable insights and foster a supportive community that understands ADHD-related work challenges.

By incorporating these additional strategies into your productivity and focus toolkit, you can address the complexities of managing ADHD with innovative solutions that cater to its unique challenges. These approaches offer a way to refine and expand your techniques, ensuring that your strategies remain effective and responsive to your evolving needs.

Career Development and Goal Setting

When it comes to advancing in your career, especially for women with ADHD, the journey is more like navigating a complex maze rather than a straightforward path. Embracing self-acceptance and cultivating a growth mindset are not just personal development tools; they are essential strategies for career progression. Here's how these elements play a crucial role in moving up the professional ladder.

Self-Acceptance: Your Foundation for Growth

First off, let's talk self-acceptance. It's the bedrock of your career advancement. Recognizing and valuing your unique ADHD traits as assets is crucial. This self-awareness becomes a springboard for identifying career opportunities that align with your strengths. For instance, if your ADHD fuels your creativity and ability to think outside conventional boundaries, roles in creative industries or innovation-driven sectors could be where you shine. By positioning your natural inclinations as assets, you position yourself for roles that not only accommodate but celebrate your unique approach to problem-solving and creativity.

Growth Mindset: The Catalyst for Career Advancement

A growth mindset, on the other hand, is your secret weapon for career advancement. It encourages resilience and adaptability—key traits for climbing the professional ladder. Viewing challenges as opportunities for growth prepares you for leadership roles, where navigating uncertainty and leading through change are daily tasks. For a woman with ADHD, this means transforming perceived setbacks or failures into lessons that forge a path forward. It's about asking, "What did I learn?" rather than dwelling on "What went wrong?" This perspective not only helps in overcoming obstacles but also showcases your capability to lead with insight and resilience, making you a valuable candidate for promotions and leadership opportunities.

Practical Steps for Career Advancement

1. **Identify Your Niche:** Use your self-knowledge to pinpoint where your ADHD traits give you an edge. Seek out roles that demand dynamism, creativity, and the ability to rapidly adapt—qualities where you naturally excel.

2. **Seek Feedback and Learn:** Embrace feedback not as criticism but as a valuable insight for growth. Continuous learning and skill development, especially in areas that might not come naturally, demonstrate your commitment to growth and excellence.

3. **Build a Supportive Network:** Surround yourself with mentors and allies who recognize your strengths and support your career goals. Networking within communities that understand the ADHD experience can also provide strategies and encouragement for navigating career challenges.

4. **Highlight Your Achievements:** Keep track of your successes and how you've uniquely contributed to your team or projects. This record is not just a confidence booster but a concrete way to demonstrate your value and readiness for advancement during performance reviews or job interviews.

By fostering self-acceptance and a growth mindset, you not only navigate your career with more resilience and confidence but also open doors to opportunities that align with your unique strengths and way of thinking. Remember, your ADHD is a part of your professional identity that, when embraced, can propel you to new heights in your career journey.

Highlights of The Chapter

Working with ADHD, especially for women, presents a unique set of challenges in the professional landscape. From battling distractions and managing time to navigating social dynamics and receiving feedback, the workplace can feel like a jungle. However, this chapter not only highlights the hurdles but also emphasizes the incredible strengths that ADHD brings to the table, such as creativity, out-of-the-box thinking, and unparalleled passion. It's about turning ADHD from a perceived obstacle into a powerful ally in your career. Understanding and embracing your ADHD means recognizing how it affects your work life and leveraging specific strategies to thrive. This includes advocating for workplace accommodations, harnessing technology for productivity, adopting flexible work schedules, and nurturing a supportive professional network. Moreover, career advancement for women with ADHD involves a deep dive into self-acceptance and a growth mindset, identifying opportunities that align with their unique skills, and continuously seeking growth and learning. By reframing the narrative around ADHD in the workplace, women can navigate their careers with confidence, turning challenges into stepping stones for success and fulfillment.

Key Points:

- **Embrace ADHD's Unique Strengths**: Recognize and utilize the creative, innovative, and passionate aspects of ADHD to enhance your work performance and satisfaction.

- **Strategize for Success**: Implement practical strategies, such as leveraging technology for organization, setting up supportive workplace accommodations, and adopting flexible schedules to maximize productivity.

- **Foster a Supportive Environment**: Advocate for yourself in the workplace, seeking accommodations that cater to your needs, and build a network of support among colleagues and mentors who understand and value your unique contributions.

- **Cultivate Self-Acceptance and Growth**: Embrace your ADHD as part of your professional identity, focusing on continuous learning and adapting to challenges with resilience and a positive outlook.

- **Navigate Career Development**: Use your self-awareness and a growth mindset to identify career paths that align with your strengths, actively seek feedback for improvement, and highlight your achievements for career advancement.

Chapter 8: Fueling the ADHD Brain

Diving right into Chapter 8, we're set to explore the ADHD brain and what it takes to keep it in top form. Imagine navigating life with ADHD as embarking on an extraordinary journey—thrilling, slightly unpredictable, but definitely rewarding. And like any good adventurer, you'll need a well-stocked toolkit. That's where exploring the benefits of a balanced diet, regular exercise, effective sleep strategies, and even some unique holistic therapies come into the picture.

This chapter isn't just another run-of-the-mill health talk or an intense workout session. Instead, we're going to have a conversation about how making small adjustments to your diet, exercise routine, and sleep habits can significantly impact managing ADHD symptoms. It's all about discovering those lifestyle tweaks that signal to your brain, "We've totally got this under control."

So, are you ready to start? Let's gear up, perhaps consider a healthy snack (though there's absolutely no obligation!), and embark on this journey to learn how nurturing both your body and mind can iron out the ADHD challenges we often face. Whether you aim to enhance your concentration, elevate your mood, or simply achieve a greater sense of harmony, rest assured, you're in the right place. Let's tackle this adventure together, shall we?

The Nourishment Connection

Let's start with the basics: fueling your body and brain. The connection between what you eat and how you feel, both physically and mentally, is profound. For women with ADHD, this relationship takes center stage. We'll explore how certain foods can act as natural allies in boosting cognitive function, enhancing focus, and stabilizing mood swings. It's not about strict diets or deprivation but discovering a pattern of eating that energizes and supports your unique brain chemistry.

What to Eat for a Brain Boost

Switching up your diet to include certain nutrients can really amp up your brain power, helping with everything from keeping your attention sharp to keeping your mood more steady:

- **Omega-3 Fatty Acids**: Super important for keeping your brain in tip-top shape, you can find omega-3s in fatty fish like salmon and trout, plus seeds like flaxseeds and chia, and even in walnuts. They're like brain food that might help you focus better and feel less jumpy or impulsive.

- **Antioxidants**: These are your brain's personal bodyguards against damage, found in tasty stuff like berries (think blueberries, strawberries, and blackberries), dark chocolate, and green leafy veggies like spinach and kale. They help keep your cognitive skills sharp and your focus on point.

- **Protein**: Getting enough good protein from foods like lean meats, fish, eggs, dairy, beans, and lentils is key for the brain chemicals that help you think and focus. Protein-packed foods can also keep your energy levels steady throughout the day, making it easier to stay on task.

- **Complex Carbohydrates**: Opting for complex carbs like whole grains, veggies, and fiber-rich fruits helps keep your blood sugar levels stable, which is great for avoiding mood swings and energy crashes. These foods provide a steady supply of energy to your brain, helping it function at its best.

The Sugar Rollercoaster

Talking about the "Sugar Rollercoaster," it's a pretty spot-on way to describe how sugary foods mess with anyone dealing with ADHD. You know, how too much sugar can send you on a wild ride of hyperactivity, lack of focus, and those all-too-familiar mood swings? Yeah, that. When your blood sugar spikes and then crashes, it's like adding fuel to the fire for those of us trying to keep our energy and attention levels on an even keel.

The Whole Sugar and ADHD Saga

So, here's the deal: Chowing down on refined sugars gives you this quick hit of energy and a mood lift. Sounds good for a hot minute, but then comes the crash—leaving you feeling tired, cranky, and even more scatterbrained. For folks with ADHD, these sugar-induced ups and downs can make our usual challenges even trickier, messing with our focus and how we're feeling throughout the day.

Smart Ways to Handle Your Sugar Fix

- **Get Clued Up**: Start by figuring out where all that

sugar in your diet is coming from. And it's not just the usual suspects like cookies and soda—sugar's sneaky and hides in places you wouldn't expect, like certain sauces and "healthy" snacks. Getting savvy about reading food labels is a game-changer.

- **Balance Is Key**: Aim for meals that mix it up with proteins, fats, and complex carbs. This trio is like the dream team for slowing down sugar's hit to your system, helping you keep your energy and mood more steady. Think an apple with some almonds—a sweet crunch with a side of chill.

- **Choose Smarter Sweets**: Got a sweet tooth? Go for treats that won't send you spiraling. Fruits, a bit of dark chocolate, or snacks sweetened with natural stuff like honey can hit the spot without the drama.

- **Water for the Win**: Sometimes, that sugar craving is just your body asking for a drink. So, before you dive into a candy bar, try having some water or a nice cup of herbal tea first. Bonus: staying hydrated is a plus for your brain, too.

- **Plan Your Treats**: Cutting out sugar completely? Not gonna happen. But if you plan for those indulgences, they're less likely to lead to a binge. Letting yourself enjoy the occasional treat means you can have your cake (now and then) and eat it too, without guilt.

- **Get Moving**: Regular exercise isn't just good for your body; it helps keep your blood sugar levels more stable, too. Plus, it's a great way to boost your mood and focus. Find an activity you love, and it won't even feel like a workout.

Beyond the Sweet Tooth

Sometimes, reaching for something sweet is more about stress or emotions than actual hunger. Figuring out what's really driving those cravings can help you find other ways to cope, like hitting pause for some deep breaths, writing it out, or getting lost in a hobby you love.

By getting smart about the sugar rollercoaster and how to ride it, women with ADHD can enjoy life's sweeter moments without letting sugar call the shots on our symptoms. It's all about finding that sweet spot where you can treat yourself without throwing your brain and body for a loop.

Hydration and ADHD

Hydration is like the unsung hero of our overall health, playing a massive role in how our brain works and how we handle our emotions. For those of us with ADHD, getting enough water becomes even more crucial. Our brains are already doing this intricate dance of managing focus and emotions, and staying hydrated is key to keeping the performance smooth.

Why Water Matters So Much for Your Brain
Think of water as the oil that keeps the engine of your body running smoothly. About 60% of you is water, and it's super important for all kinds of bodily functions, especially in your brain. If you're not drinking enough, even just a little dehydration can mess with your ability to think clearly, remember stuff, and make decisions. For someone with ADHD, who might already find these things challenging, keeping up with your water intake can really help level out those cognitive bumps.

- **Focus and Energy**: Keeping hydrated helps your brain stay on point and keep your energy up. When you're dehydrated, you might notice you're more tired and can't concentrate as well.

- **Happy Brain Chemicals**: Water is also crucial for making neurotransmitters, like dopamine and serotonin, which have a lot to do with mood and feeling rewarded. ADHD brains often need a little extra help in this department, so staying hydrated can support your mental and emotional health.

- **Cleaning House**: Drinking enough water helps flush

out toxins and waste from your brain, which means clearer thinking and better brain function. It's like giving your brain a mini detox, which is especially good for those of us navigating ADHD.

Tips for Upping Your Water Game

- **Start Your Day Right**: Kick off with a glass of water first thing in the morning. It's an easy win to get you hydrated from the get-go.

- **Keep Water Close**: Having a water bottle always by your side is a great reminder to take sips throughout the day. Pick a bottle you really like; it'll make you more likely to use it.

- **Reminder Alarms**: Forgetting to drink water is easy when you're caught up in things. Setting reminders on your phone or watch can nudge you to take hydration breaks.

- **Make Water More Fun**: Not thrilled by plain water? Jazz it up with some fruit slices, cucumber, or herbs to make it more appealing and tasty.

- **Listen to Your Body**: Get to know the signs of needing water—dry mouth, headaches, and feeling thirsty are your body's way of saying, "Hey, I need some

H2O!"

- **Eat Your Water**: Yep, you can eat your way to hydration too. Load up on fruits and veggies with high water content for an extra hydration boost.

Tapping into how hydration links up with ADHD can be a game changer in managing symptoms and boosting your brain power. With a few simple strategies, you can make sure you're getting enough water to help your focus, mood, and overall well-being stay on track.

Movement as Medicine

For women with ADHD, slipping some form of movement or exercise into daily life isn't just a bonus—it's like unlocking a secret level that boosts everything from your mood to how you tackle tasks. Exercise isn't just about getting fit; it's a key player in smoothing out those ADHD bumps, bringing clearer thinking, better emotional balance, and a nicer overall vibe to your day. Let's break down why moving your body can be such a game-changer and how to make it a fun part of your routine.

Kickstarting Your Brainpower with Exercise

Hitting the pavement, jumping on your bike, or taking a dip in the pool does more than up your heart rate. These aerobic exercises light up the parts of your brain responsible for keeping you focused, solving problems, and controlling those impulsive urges. For those of us navigating the ADHD maze, regular sweat sessions can really sharpen our focus, make finishing tasks a bit easier, and help us handle complex situations with more grace.

Shaking Off Anxiety

If anxiety is your unwanted sidekick on the ADHD journey, moving your body can be a powerful way to cut it loose. Exercise releases endorphins, those feel-good hormones that can lift your mood and melt away stress. Yoga and tai chi can be especially awesome, mixing physical movement with a dash of mindfulness to dial down anxiety and boost that inner zen.

A Natural Dopamine Detox

Getting moving isn't just great for your body—it's like a magic potion for your brain, especially if you're dealing with ADHD. Diving into a regular workout routine can seriously rev up your brain's dopamine levels. That's the good stuff that helps you feel all happy and motivated and keeps your focus laser-sharp. For folks with ADHD, who might have a bit of a rollercoaster relationship with dopamine, adding some action-packed exercise into the mix can be a game-changer, kind of like hitting the reset button on your brain's dopamine stash. When you get your heart pumping, your body starts churning out more dopamine, that key player behind the awesome feels you get after crushing a workout. For someone with ADHD, this natural dopamine boost can mean better moods, more get-up-and-go, and crisper focus.

Discovering the Fun in Fitness

Transforming exercise into a part of your day that you genuinely look forward to is like rediscovering the joy of play. It's about shifting the view of exercise from being a dreaded task on your to-do list to an exciting activity that's as fun as recess used to be when we were kids. The secret? Finding ways to make physical activity mesh with your interests and personality, so it feels less like a mandatory chore and more like the best part of your day. Imagine dancing to your favorite tunes, not just as a form of exercise but as a way to express yourself and enjoy the music you love. There's a kind of magic in dance that allows you to let loose, whether you're in a structured class like Zumba, showing off your hip-hop moves, or just freestyling in your living room.

Then there's the call of the great outdoors, appealing to the adventurer in you. Whether it's hiking up a mountain, biking down a winding trail, or taking a leisurely stroll in the park, being outside offers a workout for your body and a refreshing reset for your mind. It turns exercise into an exploration, where every step is about enjoying the moment and the world around you.

For those seeking a quieter but equally powerful form of movement, yoga offers a serene escape, balancing physical challenge with mental relaxation. It's an exercise in mindfulness as much as it is in physicality, inviting you to find peace and flexibility in both your body and mind.

And let's not forget the thrill of team sports, which combine the joy of physical activity with the fun of social interaction. Whether it's the camaraderie of a soccer team, the friendly competition of a tennis match, or the collective effort of a volleyball game, sports have a way of making you forget you're working out at all.

But how do you keep the excitement alive in your fitness routine? The key is in mixing things up and keeping it fresh, setting playful goals that challenge you in new and enjoyable ways, and maybe even involving friends or family in your active pursuits. It's about creating an exercise routine that doesn't feel routine at all, one that you're genuinely excited to dive into. Rewarding yourself for staying active can also help, linking positive experiences with your fitness journey and reinforcing the habit.

In essence, making exercise enjoyable is about embracing the fun in movement, allowing that joy to guide you to a healthier, happier you. It's about looking forward to your next workout not because you have to, but because you want to, and because it's genuinely the best part of your day.

Crafting the Perfect Plan

Fitting exercise into your life in a way that feels doable is all about striking the right balance. Setting up a kind of flexible routine—like planning to move around the same time each day—can help make exercise a regular thing without feeling boxed in. Mixing up your activities can keep boredom at bay and make sure you're always looking forward to what's next, all while adapting to how you're feeling and what you're up for on any given day.

In a nutshell, getting into exercise can be a total game-changer for women with ADHD, transforming it from a should-do into a totally-worth-it adventure that spices up your daily routine, sharpens your mind, and lifts your spirits.

Highlights of The Chapter

Chapter 8 unfolds as an enlightening journey into optimizing the ADHD brain through lifestyle adjustments, focusing on the pillars of diet, exercise, sleep, and holistic therapies. It's a dialogue about transforming daily routines into powerful strategies for managing ADHD symptoms, enhancing focus, mood, and overall well-being. This isn't just a chapter on health; it's a guide to unlocking the full potential of the ADHD mind by nurturing the body with mindful nutrition, engaging physical activity, restorative sleep practices, and complementary holistic approaches. The goal is to equip women with ADHD with a toolkit that not only addresses the challenges but also celebrates the unique advantages of their neurodiverse brains, enabling them to navigate life with confidence, resilience, and joy.

Key Points:

- **Nutrition as a Foundation**: Emphasizes the significant impact of a balanced diet on ADHD symptoms, highlighting the brain-boosting benefits of omega-3 fatty acids, antioxidants, protein, and complex carbohydrates, while advising moderation in sugar intake to avoid exacerbating symptoms.

- **The Power of Movement**: Details how regular exercise, from aerobic activities to yoga, can enhance cognitive function, reduce anxiety, and naturally balance dopamine levels, offering practical tips for integrating enjoyable physical activity into daily life.

- **Sleep Strategies for ADHD**: Outlines the crucial role of quality sleep in managing ADHD symptoms and provides actionable advice for establishing effective sleep routines and habits to ensure restorative rest.

- **Holistic Therapies and Mindfulness**: Explores the benefits of complementary therapies, such as meditation, mindfulness practices, and potentially beneficial supplements, in achieving mental clarity, emotional balance, and a heightened sense of well-being.

- **Practical Lifestyle Adjustments**: Offers a range of strategies for incorporating these pillars into everyday life, from smart dietary choices and fun exercise routines to prioritizing sleep and exploring holistic practices, all tailored to the unique needs of women with ADHD.

- **Empowerment Through Self-Care**: Encourages women with ADHD to view these lifestyle adjustments not as chores, but as empowering acts of self-care that honor their neurodiversity and support their journey toward personal and professional fulfillment.

Chapter 9: Harnessing Your Strengths

Alright, lovely humans, we've journeyed through the twists and turns of ADHD together, unpacking challenges, strategies, and real-talk advice. Now, we're at the heart of it all—the grand finale where we celebrate the sparkle and shine of ADHD. This chapter is your standing ovation, a tribute to the incredible strengths and beauty that come with living with ADHD. It's about flipping the script from focusing solely on the hurdles to basking in the glow of your unique gifts.

ADHD isn't just a list of symptoms to manage; it's a part of who you are, weaving threads of creativity, empathy, and resilience into the fabric of your being. Here, we're not just coping or adapting; we're thriving, leveraging the innate strengths that ADHD blesses us with. It's about recognizing the superpowers hidden in plain sight and using them to craft a life that's as vibrant and dynamic as you are.

We'll dive into the traits that make ADHD folks some of the most innovative, passionate, and intuitive souls walking this planet. From the ability to think outside the box to the capacity for deep, boundless passion in pursuits that light a fire in our hearts. It's these qualities that often lead to breakthroughs, innovations, and the kind of art, ideas, and movements that change the world.

But let's not skirt around the fact that with these strengths can come a battle with self-esteem. Society's got a narrow view of what success and normalcy look like, and it's high time we bust those myths wide open. This chapter is also your toolkit for building and nurturing a rock-solid sense of self-worth, grounded in the understanding and appreciation of your ADHD brain.

So, get comfy, and let's celebrate the journey, the challenges, and most importantly, the incredible strengths that come with ADHD. It's time to own your story, your struggles, and your successes. You're not just navigating life with ADHD; you're mastering the art of leveraging it to its fullest, creating a life that's as unique and extraordinary as you.

Identifying and Leveraging Personal Strengths

The first step in leveraging your strengths is to identify them. This can be a reflective process, requiring you to look inward and perhaps reassess past experiences through a new lens. Consider moments when you felt most alive, engaged, or proud of your accomplishments. These are clues to your inherent strengths. Women with ADHD often find that their strengths lie in creativity, empathy, resilience, and dynamic problem-solving abilities.

- **Creativity**: Your creativity is like your superpower, letting you see the world in ways no one else does and coming up with ideas that fly under everyone else's radar. This knack for creativity isn't just about being artsy; it's your secret sauce for tackling everyday challenges with a fresh twist. Whether you're flipping a boring task on its head or cracking a tough problem with a stroke of genius, your creative mind shows you're not one to stick to the beaten path. Recognizing this means seeing the incredible value your creativity brings not just to art but to all those moments that benefit from a spark of original thinking.

- **Empathy**: Then there's empathy, your ability to really get where people are coming from on an emotional level. It's more than just being nice; it's a deep-seated power that helps you forge strong, meaningful connections. This empathy makes you someone people turn to for support and guidance, creating spaces filled with understanding and care. By valuing this gift, you see how it enriches your relationships and brings a genuine sense of connection to both your personal life and work environment.

- **Resilience**: Resilience is another badge of honor your ADHD journey has given you. It's not just about getting back up when life knocks you down; it's about your unmatched ability to adapt, find new ways forward, and keep pushing through when things get tough. This resilience is a clear sign of your strength, showing you can take on life's hurdles with confidence and keep moving forward. Embracing your resilience means seeing it as the powerhouse it truly is, giving you the courage to tackle any challenge that comes your way.

- **Dynamic Problem-Solving**: And let's not forget about your dynamic approach to problem-solving. Your brain's always on the move, juggling different ideas, switching up viewpoints, and coming up with clever solutions on the fly. This ability is a game-changer, making you a pro at navigating both the little bumps and big challenges life throws at you. Recognizing this talent means appreciating your unique way of thinking and applying it across all areas of your life where thinking fast, being flexible, and innovating are key.

Exercise: Uncovering Your ADHD Strengths

Objective: To deepen your understanding and appreciation of your unique strengths as a woman with ADHD, leading to greater self-esteem and empowerment.

Materials Needed: A comfortable and quiet space, a notebook, and a pen or pencil.

Duration: Set aside about 1-2 hours for thorough reflection. This exercise doesn't have to be completed in one sitting; feel free to take breaks and return to it as needed.

Part 1: Strengths Discovery

1. Rapid Ideation and Creative Problem-Solving:

- When have you come up with a solution to a problem that nobody else thought of? Describe the problem and your unique solution.

- Reflect on a time when you had to think on your feet. What was the situation, and what was your response?

2. Intense Focus (Hyperfocus):

- Describe a project or task where you experienced hyperfocus. What were you working on, and what did you accomplish during this state?

- How can you channel your ability to hyperfocus into areas of your life or work that you are passionate about?

3. Resilience and Perseverance:

- Think of a situation where you faced significant obstacles or setbacks. How did you overcome these challenges?

- What does resilience mean to you, and how have you demonstrated it in your personal or professional life?

4. Empathy and Intuitive Understanding:

- Recall a time when you sensed what someone else was feeling without them having to tell you. How did you respond?

- How has your empathy or intuition positively impacted your relationships or interactions with others?

Part 2: Strengths Mapping

1. Skills and Talents Inventory:

- List all the skills and talents you believe you possess. Include everything, no matter how small or significant it might seem.

- Next to each skill or talent, write down an example of how you have used or demonstrated this in real-life situations.

2. The ADHD Advantage:

- For each of the strengths identified in Part 1, write down how having ADHD has contributed to these strengths. Consider how your ADHD traits enhance these abilities or offer a unique perspective.

Part 3: Application and Growth

1. Setting Strengths-Based Goals:

- Choose three strengths you want to focus on and develop further. For each, set a specific goal that leverages this strength in a positive and constructive way.

- Outline actionable steps to achieve these goals. Consider any support or resources you might need.

2. Overcoming Challenges With Strengths:

- Identify potential challenges or areas of difficulty in your life. How can you use your identified strengths to address or mitigate these challenges?

- Create a plan that outlines how you will apply your strengths to overcome these obstacles.

Part 4: Reflection and Commitment

- Reflect on this exercise and the insights you've gained about your strengths. How do you feel about these strengths now?

- Write a commitment to yourself on how you will use and celebrate these strengths moving forward. This could be a daily affirmation, a weekly review of how you've used your strengths, or any other ritual that helps you acknowledge and grow your abilities.

This exercise is designed to provide a deeper and more structured exploration of your strengths, specifically tailored to the unique experiences of women with ADHD. By focusing on concrete examples and actionable plans, it aims to empower you to recognize and utilize your strengths in all areas of your life.

Celebrating and Sharing Your Strengths

Diving into the whirlwind journey of self-discovery as a woman with ADHD is kind of like unlocking a secret level in the game of life. It's not just about getting to know yourself better; it's a full-on mission to shine a spotlight on those unique strengths that often get overshadowed by the ADHD hustle. This isn't just some fluffy, feel-good exercise. It's a crucial step toward grabbing life by the horns and steering it in a direction that celebrates who you truly are.

Spotlight on Your Superpowers
Let's talk about putting your strengths center stage. If you've got a knack for creativity, it's about seeing the world in vibrant colors and patterns that others might miss, turning even the mundane into something magical. And hey, if you can feel what others are feeling almost as if it's your own emotion, that's your empathy superpower at work. It's about turning those deep connections into something tangible that can uplift those around you.

And resilience? If you've got ADHD, chances are you've got resilience in spades. It's that gritty determination that gets you through the tough spots, ready to bounce back stronger every time. Then there's your dynamic problem-solving – your brain's fantastic ability to juggle ideas, flip perspectives, and come up with solutions on the fly. It's like having a mental Swiss Army knife that's ready for any challenge.

Shine, Baby, Shine

Now, how do you take these killer strengths and make them work for you? It's about seeking out those golden opportunities to show the world what you're made of. Got a gift for gab? Light up the stage with your insights and stories. Passionate about a cause or a project? Lead the charge and let your creativity and drive pave the way. And when it comes to sharing your thoughts, remember, your unique viewpoint can spark the kind of innovation and inclusivity the world desperately needs. Mentoring is where you get to pass on the wisdom of your journey, offering a hand to those coming up behind you. It's not just about guiding others; it's a reminder of how far you've come and a chance to reinforce your own superpowers. Especially for other women with ADHD, your story can be a beacon of hope, a reminder that they're not alone and that incredible things are within reach.

Embrace Your Narrative

Owning your ADHD journey and the strengths that come with it is a bold statement of self-acceptance and empowerment. It's about changing the tired old narrative of ADHD from something to overcome to something that enriches your perspective and approach to life. This mindset shift is powerful – it not only fuels your growth and happiness but also chips away at stereotypes, paving the way for a more understanding and diverse world. By leaning into and sharing your unique strengths, you're doing so much more than just carving out a successful path for yourself. You're setting the stage for a life that's rich with purpose, passion, and impact. Your journey shines a light on the untapped potential within ADHD, inspiring others and broadening the understanding of what it means to live and thrive with ADHD.

Remember, ADHD comes with a spectrum of experiences, challenges, and yes, superpowers. As women navigating this path, we're uniquely equipped to explore and celebrate the full range of what ADHD brings to our lives. By embracing our strengths, we're not just bettering our own lives; we're contributing to a world that values the diverse talents of everyone. Let's make it happen – together.

Highlights of The Chapter

As we wrap up our exploration of living with ADHD, particularly for women, we celebrate not just the journey but the extraordinary strengths that come with it. ADHD is more than a set of challenges; it's a reservoir of creativity, empathy, resilience, and dynamic problem-solving abilities that enrich our lives and those around us. This chapter isn't just a conclusion; it's a standing ovation for the unique gifts ADHD bestows upon us, urging us to see beyond the hurdles and recognize the incredible advantages our neurodiversity offers.

Key Points:

- **Embrace Your Creativity**: Your creative flair is a superpower, allowing you to see and solve problems in innovative ways that others might overlook. It's about harnessing this creativity to not only navigate life's challenges but to enrich the world with your unique perspectives and solutions.

- **Leverage Your Empathy**: The deep empathy characteristic of many women with ADHD is a strength that fosters strong, meaningful connections. It's a tool for building relationships based on understanding and compassion, making you a cherished friend, family member, and colleague.

- **Build on Your Resilience**: The resilience honed through navigating life with ADHD is a testament to your strength. It's about recognizing this resilience as a foundation for overcoming obstacles and pursuing your goals with determination and grace.

- **Utilize Dynamic Problem-Solving**: Your ability to think on your feet and approach problems from unique angles is invaluable. It's about applying this dynamic problem-solving skill across various aspects of your life, turning potential challenges into opportunities for growth and innovation.

- **Cultivate Self-Worth and Confidence**: Building and nurturing a strong sense of self-worth is crucial. It's about viewing your ADHD not as a flaw but as a part of your identity that brings valuable strengths and perspectives to the table.

- **Share Your Journey**: By sharing your story and the strengths you've discovered along the way, you contribute to a broader understanding of ADHD. It's about inspiring others and highlighting the diverse talents that come with neurodiversity.

Conclusion

And just like that, we're turning the last page of this journey together. It's been quite the adventure, hasn't it? Exploring the ins and outs of living with ADHD, especially from our lens as women, has been both enlightening and empowering. As we wrap things up, let's take a moment to sit back and reflect on everything we've discovered and shared.

First things first: give yourself a massive pat on the back. Seriously, navigating through the maze of ADHD is no small feat, and you've been an absolute champ. We've tackled the tough stuff together – emotional ups and downs, those sneaky time management pitfalls, and even the tricky bits about money and relationships. Keep these gems in your back pocket; they're your go-to tools for when life throws its curveballs.

Now, let's get something straight – your ADHD? It's not a glitch; it's your superpower. Yeah, it can be a bit wild and a whole lot unpredictable, but it's also the source of your unique strengths – your creativity, your empathy, and that boundless energy that can light up a room.

What's the game plan from here? It's simple: embrace your ADHD and make it work for you. Think of it as your very own wildcard – a bit unexpected, sure, but oh-so-powerful when played right. And if you stumble? No sweat. Every misstep is just a new learning moment, a chance to dust yourself off and jump back in with even more gusto.

Remember, this journey with ADHD isn't a solo mission. There's a whole squad of us out there, all navigating this same wild ride. We're here to back you up, share a laugh, and celebrate every victory along the way, big or small.

This book isn't just a one-time read. Let it be your go-to guide when things get tough, or when you need a reminder of how kickass you are. And your story? It's worth its weight in gold. Share it far and wide because the world could use a bit more of that ADHD magic.

So, what's next? Just take a deep breath and dive into your life with all the gusto you've got. Embrace the chaos, find joy in the little victories, and never stop being your awesome, ADHD self.

As we wrap this up, remember: life with ADHD is a wild, wonderful adventure. Sure, it's got its challenges, but it's also filled with incredible moments of brilliance and creativity. You've got everything you need to make this journey an amazing one.

Keep shining, keep being you, and keep rocking that ADHD. The world is so much brighter with your unique spark in it. And hey, who knows what amazing things you'll do next? The possibilities are endless.

So, off you go. Keep living life in your fabulous, slightly ADHD way. Here's to all the adventures ahead – may they be as unique and wonderful as you are.

www.ingramcontent.com/pod-product-compliance
Lightning Source LLC
LaVergne TN
LVHW021818060526
838201LV00058B/3427